All I'm Created to Be

to Be

Set Free!

Faith-based Guided Journaling for Adult Children of Dysfunctional Families

Patricia Johnson-Laster, B.A., M.A., M.R.E., Ed.D.

WESTBOW
PRESS®
A DIVISION OF THOMAS NELSON
& ZONDERVAN

WestBow Press books may be ordered through booksellers or by contacting:

WestBow Press
A Division of Thomas Nelson & Zondervan
1663 Liberty Drive
Bloomington, IN 47403
www.westbowpress.com
1 (866) 928-1240

ISBN: 978-1-9736-0191-3 (sc)
ISBN: 978-1-9736-0190-6 (e)

Print information available on the last page.

WestBow Press rev. date: 09/18/2017

All I'm Created to Be

Set Free!

Patricia Johnson-Laster, B.A.,M.A.,M.R.E.,ED.D.

Contents

Section Two: Rising From The Ashes

INTRODUCTION

Personal and spiritual growth are lifetime processes: vibrant, exhilarating, demanding, and fun. They also include painful moments of self-examination and stretching, especially for those who bring unresolved childhood issues into the process. This workbook offers psychologically and Biblically-based guided journaling to help readers resolve issues left from their childhood, grow spiritually and gain confidence. Each of the ten steps includes four to six exercises; and each exercise is made up of four components: case histories, "Spiritual Prep" (Scripture study), journaling, and related activities. Case histories are derived from my work with students and colleagues. All names have been changed.

It's my hope that, after reading the brief reflection on each topic, the reader will begin his or her own journey toward personal and spiritual fulfillment by completing the Scripture readings provided, responding fully (and in writing) to the questions, and engaging in the suggested activities. Reading, journaling, and Scripture study may also be done in a supportive group setting. A group leader does not need special training. For more details on how to conduct a group, see the appendix, "Leading an 'All I'm Created to be: Set Free' Small Group." In a group setting, members' responses should be voluntary, and confidentiality should be honored by everyone in the group.

Although the workbook allows the reader to proceed at his or her own pace, it's suggested that at least one day or more be given to work through each exercise. This would provide optimal opportunity to deal with and move beyond the issues covered in a particular exercise. Because of the confidential and personal nature of this workbook, you may want to keep it in a safe place.

Family Patterns

A very common misconception of a dysfunctional family is that the parents are always on the verge of separation and divorce. Frequently, individuals from unhealthy families grow up thinking their families were fully functional, normal, even exceptional, especially if their parents had strong marital and emotional bonds. This is not necessarily true. Let's examine the continuum of family treatment ranging from normal, healthy families to abusive ones.

Healthy families are not perfect. There may be times when there is bickering, yelling, hurt feelings, anger, and misunderstanding, but these are the exception rather than the rule. Healthy families have a consistent core of love, mutual respect, and common values. Parents are the teachers and leaders of the family. There is no role reversal between parent and child, but parents lead by example and encourage open, honest communication. Each member is valued as an individual and not forced to conform to another family member's demands. Discussion, differences of opinion, emotional expression are all allowed and accepted. Family rules are explicit and consistent, but flexible enough to allow for individual needs and situations. Each member is encouraged to pursue his or her own interests.

Dysfunctional parenting lies on the continuum between healthy and abusive parenting. Some of the more generally recognized characteristics of dysfunctional families include:

- An imbalance of negative, harsh, controlling childrearing methods relative to positive ones
- A refusal to admit there's a problem. The dysfunctional family tries to appear normal and even exceptional.
- Parents do not allow perceptions or feelings which contradict their own.
- Scapegoating of one particular family member with the message "You are the reason for everything that is bad or wrong." The scapegoat is made to carry the hidden blame for any family problem.
- A shifting of reality between what is said and what is actually happening (i.e., a get-together is described as a "great time" when actually it was a disaster)
- Over-controlling, intrusive parenting, and failure to recognize the child's individuality, leading to inadequate or inappropriate boundaries
- Family members being played against each other
- Unrealistic expectations and rigid, inflexible rules

Abusive parenting is distinct from dysfunctional parenting in the degree of severity, risk of harm to the child, and imbalance. Abusive parenting is an appalling, extreme, disturbing form of verbal abuse, mental cruelty, physical and/or sexual abuse, and neglect which requires intervention to protect the children from actual harm. *Please note*: This book is designed to facilitate the healing process for adults with issues from their childhood and/or who experienced moderate forms of dysfunctional families. If you experienced abuse as a child, this book in itself is not intended as sufficient help. Consider contacting a therapist or counselor with expertise in working with adult children of abusive families to guide you as you work through this book.

As preparation for the work in this book, the following list of family dysfunctional patterns is presented here. Before beginning your own personal journey, try to identify any dysfunctional patterns of behavior that might have characterized some of your family members. *If you are using "All I'm Created to be: Set Free" in a group setting, this exercise is for your information only and is to be completed prior to beginning group work. It is not to be disclosed in the group setting.* Circle those that apply to your family history. If you would like, within the parenthesis abbreviate the name or relationship of the person who demonstrated that characteristic. Add additional terms you feel are needed:

Manipulating	(	)	Disapproving	(	)
Shaming	(	)	Teasing	(	)
Controlling	(	)	Laughing at	(	)
Overprotective	(	)	Not taking seriously	(	)
Intrusive	(	)	Misleading	(	)
Inflicting guilt	(	)	Overpowering/bullying	(	)
Degrading	(	)	Breaking promises	(	)
Deceptive	(	)	Emotionally absent	(	)
Patronizing	(	)	Public-image managers	(	)
Always negative	(	)	Taboo enforcers	(	)
Dominating	(	)	Critical	(	)
Blackmailing	(	)	Narcissistic	(	)
Name-calling	(	)	Judgmental	(	)
Denial	(	)	Unforgiving	(	)
Users	(	)	Blaming	(	)
Dogmatic	(	)	Belittling	(	)

SECTION ONE

Ashes On Fertile Ground

STEP ONE

When Only Ashes Are Left

Exercise 1

....

OUT FROM BEHIND THE MASK

The Lord does not look at the things people look at. People look at the outward appearance, but the Lord looks at the heart.
1 Samuel 16:7, NIV

Anna approached my desk one day after a class discussion on parenting and asked if she could talk with me. That chat turned into many as she revealed her story. Anna told me that her birth was a late-in-life accident and not welcomed. In a family increasingly plagued with problems, Anna was made the target for blame. She was repeatedly given the message that she was the reason for anything and everything that went wrong within the family:

"Shame on you...."

"It's all your fault...."

"Don't be like that...."

"You caused it...."

"You're just like your (name of disliked relative)...."

"You're making that up...."

"I should never have had you...."

"You think you're so smart...."

Anna could never be good enough. Even when she excelled at something, her achievements were disregarded or she was made to feel that, somehow, she cheated. Anna endured regular putdowns and behind-her-back betrayals. She was labeled "bad" and was made the buffer against

1

the reality that theirs was a troubled family. Other family members were affirmed for their agreement that Anna was at fault for whatever went wrong.

As a young adult, Anna was weighed down with an overwhelming sense of inferiority. The first time I met her, Anna's behavior, mannerisms, and conversation bore the marks of someone crippled with guilt and shame. Because she believed that no one could possibly like her if they knew what she was really like, Anna withdrew and learned to hide her deepest thoughts and feelings even from herself. Instead, she used her sensitivity and keen intelligence to tune into other people's feelings about her and tried to be whatever they wanted. But it wasn't her; it was a mask she wore.

During her college years, Anna continued to drop by my office to chat. She worked hard to overcome her low self-esteem and develop more confidence in herself. We talked about how she could trust God's love for her, and as she began to exercise that trust, she started to value the person she really was. Little by little she put away the various masks she was tempted to wear. Anna knows that it will be a lifelong effort to be true to herself. But as she and I both agreed years ago, the point is to try, to keep on trying, and to never give up.

As a psychologist and a Christian, I've come to profoundly believe that faith is a critical and an essential component to complete healing. Many of the case histories in this workbook point to faith, Bible study, and prayer as the key to finding answers. There are no quick fixes, no bandages, no matter how much we desire them, that provide an instant cure. The exercises and questions provided in the "All I'm Created to Be" and "Set Free" sections of the workbook are designed to help you begin the process of healing but it's my firm belief as a psychologist, that only God can fully bring a person to be all that he or she was created to be.

Thank goodness God can see beyond outward appearances! To know ourselves, to become a person who is whole and consistent in motive and appearance may be one of the most difficult tasks we encounter on our pilgrimage. It involves growing in awareness and acceptance of who we are, of what we think and feel. It means working through and then putting aside past hurts, misunderstandings, and betrayals. This book is designed to help. If you make the effort, God will be with you each step of the way.

Spiritual Prep: *Psalms 51:6; John 7:24; 2 Corinthians 4:16; Ephesians 3:14–19; I Thessalonians 5:23–24*

All I'm Created to be

My favorite things are (do not censor yourself here but jot down anything and everything that comes to mind):

On gray, rainy days, I enjoy:

On a beautiful sunny day, I like to:

I feel most like myself when:

I feel least like myself when:

This is the way other people see me:

This is the secret self that I don't let others see:

Set Free

Find a photograph of yourself as a child and tape or glue it to the inside of the front cover of this workbook. That child is still a part of you. Each day, take a few minutes to study the photograph and say a prayer for the child in it. Allow our Heavenly Father to show you how much He loves the child in the photograph. Absorb that love. Continue this exercise throughout your use of this book.

Prayer: Lord, help me to get in touch with my authentic feelings and thoughts. Help me to face, deal with, and then forget past wrongs as I become the authentic Christ-in-me person You created me to be.

Exercise 2

....

UNMET NEEDS

*But whatever were gains to me I now consider loss for the sake of Christ. What is more, I
consider everything a loss because of the surpassing worth of knowing Christ Jesus my Lord.*
Philippians 3:7–8, NIV

Matt had the small group laughing as he described how he gathered a bunch of daisies for his friend, Emily, and placed them on the front seat of her car. "What a nice surprise they'll be," he thought. The only problem was that it was a miserably hot summer day and, with the sun beating down on the roof of the car, the flowers wilted. All Emily found was a terribly dreary bunch of stems and shriveled daisy petals. "Emily and I had a good laugh over those wilted flowers, but they reminded me of something," Matt said as his mood turned serious. "No matter how hard I work, it just seems that any mistake, any misunderstanding, any critical remark from a friend, makes me feel like my life is like that dreary bunch of dried-up weeds and shriveled petals. Sometimes I just want to give up."

Matt's parents divorced when Matt was only a toddler; after the divorce, Matt's mom became depressed, bitter, and resentful of having to raise a child alone. For a long time, Matt thought it was his fault that his dad had left, especially since his father didn't want any more to do with them once he was gone. Matt remembers trying to be "strong" for his Mom and feeling lonely a lot, but he had trouble recalling times that he felt truly loved. Later, when Matt was chatting with me in my office, I asked him to explain further his comments about the shriveled flowers. "I remember trying to help my mom because she was so depressed. I felt like I had to be the adult, to be a 'big man' for her but I could never do enough to make her happy. I really felt overwhelmed as a child and still feel that way sometimes." Matt's insecurity and desperate need drove him to higher and higher efforts to gain the love and attention that was missing from his childhood. He was repeatedly caught in a trap of working to gain what he so desperately needed. Matt explained that he knew, rationally, that God loved him; however, he felt so undeserving of it, so empty, that God seemed too distant to help. Actually, he admitted, he frequently wondered whether God loved him at all.

Despite doubting God's love for him, Matt persisted in his faith and, over the next few years, I watched Matt evolve into a calmer, more tranquil person. God's patience and love seem to forge its way deeper into Matt's heart and life. In one of our last chats, as graduation and Matt's wedding date to Emily drew near, Matt talked with me about what led to the change in his life. His persistent study of Scripture and devotional time helped Matt realize that he could trust God's love regardless of whether he felt loved or not. Through the affirmation of Christian friends, teachers, and counselors whom God brought into his life, Matt gradually began to understand how much God loved him. Matt told me that he came to realize that, deprived of the affection and attention he needed as a child, he was still trying to get those needs met. He said that when he finally started to accept that God knew and cared about his unmet needs and the pain he carried, Matt was able to loosen his grasp and let God start to heal his heart with God's perfect love and acceptance. As Matt's daily walk with Him deepened, so did Matt's awareness that God, alone, was adequate to fill his unmet needs.

Let me point out that it is certainly not unhealthy to cherish love, acceptance, recognition and respect from others. I believe that God reinforces how much He loves us by bringing individuals into our lives who care for and accept us. Yet, while we need and enjoy the attention of others, the driving force of an authentic Christian's life is God's love. As Matt discovered, nothing surpasses the awareness of God's love and the joy of His presence as we daily walk with Him.

Spiritual Prep: *Deuteronomy 33:27a; Proverbs 3:21–26; 14:26; Jeremiah 31:3; John 14:12; Hebrews 4:16*

All I'm Created to be

Look over the following list of needs and check those that were adequately met for you as a child. Read the list again and highlight (circle or note with colored marker) the needs that did not get met in your childhood.

_____basic physical needs such as food, water, and sleep

_____care and comfort when physically sick and/or ill

_____touching, hugs and human contact

_____feeling safe

_____feeling secure

_____nurturing

_____unconditional love

_____attention

_____listening

_____support

_____trust

_____belongingness

_____freedom to become

_____freedom to express yourself

_____acceptance

_____recognition

_____respect

Set Free

If I could have anything I needed or wanted as I grew up, but didn't have, it would be:

Prayer: Lord Jesus, show me my worth and value in Your eyes.

Exercise 3

....

FAILURE TO ESTABLISH BOUNDARIES

You have searched me, Lord, and you know me. You know when I
sit and when I rise; you perceive my thoughts from afar.
Psalm 139:1–2, NIV

Establishing boundaries within a relationship is a popular and important topic which we'll discuss in a later exercise. First, however, we need to recognize that in any healthy lifestyle, boundaries are needed for one's own behavior. This doesn't mean that we have to live a limited, restrictive lifestyle, but it does mean that we exercise self-control. When we establish boundaries for ourselves, we take responsibility for our thoughts, habits, emotions, and behaviors. The ability to establish and set boundaries for one's own behavior illustrates a mastery over our desires and appetites. It reflects an inner strength. Self-discipline helps us to overcome such behaviors as violent gestures, self-harming, explosive anger, rage, workaholism, gambling, binging and purging, excessive drinking or drug use, and reckless sexual behavior. Self-control gives us the power to stick to our decisions and follow them through.

Jennifer had a beautiful testimony and she shared it with me on a Friday afternoon when her classes were finished for the week. As she began her story, Jennifer made it clear that she had wonderful parents and wondered why she, herself, had made so many destructive choices.

Jennifer's parents were devoted to their career goals and, as Jennifer thought more about her childhood, she remembered they had little energy left for involvement in her childhood activities. They pacified Jennifer by giving her anything she wanted and permitted her to do whatever she desired. They were lax and undemanding. As parents, they rarely exerted any control over Jennifer's behavior and made few demands of her. Jennifer was allowed to act on her impulses without either positive or negative consequences. She was given few boundaries and received little, if any, discipline.

Jennifer was smart but performed poorly in school. She was impulsive and generally not liked by her peers. Desperate to gain friends, Jennifer made self-destructive choices involving drugs, promiscuity, and when all else failed, attempts at suicide. There seem to be no depth to which she wouldn't sink—until she met Alex. Alex was a strong Christian who took an interest in Jennifer and invited her to his church. Grateful for his friendship, Jennifer began to attend and participate in the youth group at Alex's church. There, she accepted Christ into her life.

Jennifer continued to falter and make bad choices. Yet God never gave up on her. God let her know repeatedly that no matter what she did, He was with her. He was always ready to forgive her and help her grow. The study of His word led Jennifer to see a need to develop new goals and exercise more self-control. Jennifer pulled her grades up and formed healthier relationships. In doing this, Jennifer began to regard herself as a person with dignity and value. By the time I met her, Jennifer was able to hold her head high and her shoulders back and face the world with confidence. God had taught her this.

The search for self is one we all must travel, but it's an individual pilgrimage. If you are just now embarking on this journey, here are some things that might help you:

- Turn to God daily in private prayer and Scripture study as you read this book.
- Under His guidance, set goals for your life.
- Prayerfully establish boundaries for what you will and will not do.
- Seek out resources you need—books, counselors, leaders in your church—to help you sustain the boundaries you set and reach your goals.

If you faithfully set aside time each day to spend talking with and listening to God, reading His word, He will shed light on your search for self. No one can make this pilgrimage for you, but never doubt that it's an honorable one. God wants you to know yourself and to set the boundaries and goals that your life needs. An unexamined, shallow sense of identity with no boundaries nor goals accounts for much of the unhappiness and superficiality found in the lives of many Christians. Don't give up. God wants you to accept and assume responsibility for yourself. He wants you to love yourself as He loves you.

Spiritual Prep: *2 Samuel 22:29–31; Psalm 19:12-14; Proverbs 14:8; Jeremiah 9:23–24; 1 Corinthians 2:9–12*

All I'm Created to be

Describe your father:

Describe your mother:

Set Free

1. Identify and list five goals for your life.

2. List some unacceptable activities that are outside the boundaries for the life you would like to live:

3. List those activities you enjoy doing that are within the boundaries you set for your life:

Reminder: Are you continuing the special exercise you began in the first step of this chapter? Did you find a photograph of yourself as a child and attach it to the inside cover of this workbook where you can see it each day? Continue, when you see the photograph of yourself as a child, to pause, pray, and absorb the love which God had and has for you as His child.

Prayer: Father, I give my heart and life to you. Please show me the path you want me to take, guide my steps, and keep me strong in my faith.

Exercise 4

....

DISCOURAGEMENT

Therefore encourage one another and build each other up.
1Thessalonians 5:11, NIV

Kinsey was the first born in a family of five children. Her parents were pressured to marry quite young and were not fully prepared for raising a child. Since they came from a very authoritarian home with domineering parents themselves, they followed the only example they knew for raising Kinsey. Young and immature, Kinsey's parents felt they were doing a good job of parenting by following that example.

Kinsey was given rigid rules and high expectations before she could even walk. She was tested and then punished if she failed the tests. Kinsey could remember Christmas presents being placed within her reach around the house which she was not to touch; if she did so, she received a whipping with a small metal rod. Because she was a curious, inquisitive child, she received quite a lot of those whippings. When a concerned visitor asked her parents why they laid objects around if they didn't want Kinsey to touch them, her parents replied that this was the way to teach her to obey them.

Kinsey's early childhood was one of learning to obey a long list of inflexible rules. No excuse was permitted for disobeying any rule, and no disagreement with her parents was tolerated. Kinsey was expected to act "like a young adult" and to never argue with her parents. If she attempted to express an opinion which differed the least from theirs, she was mocked, isolated, or made to feel guilty.

Like her parents before her, Kinsey entered her middle-school years a replica of her Mom and Dad. Her individuality had been successfully snuffed out. By her teen years, she had given up trying to discover the unique, special individual she was, stopped questioning her parents at all, and never had an opinion differing from theirs or from any authoritarian figure. If her ideas did differ from those in authority, she felt such self doubt, guilt, and shame that she couldn't express the opinion. Her discomfort was obvious whenever any of her teachers asked her to express her own opinions. Kinsey had grown comfortable in her silence and was amazed that her friends in college would question, let alone disagree with, her professors.

While at college, Kinsey had a devoutly religious friend who was a passionate follower of a well-known cult. Once introduced, Kinsey was drawn to the cult leader. The last I heard of Kinsey, she'd been cut off from her parents, her world, and any life outside of the cult. Kinsey's parents mourned her loss from their family with frustration and anger, never grasping why their perfect daughter could follow a cult leader so blindly.

Spiritual Prep: Before reading the Scripture verses in this section, read the following explanation of two key words, "rod" and "discipline." Once you've read the explanation of these words, then read *Proverbs 13:24; Proverbs 22:15;* and *Proverbs 29:15;* and decide how you would interpret those verses in light of this information.

A rod was a staff used by a shepherd to gently guide his sheep and pull them out of danger. It was not common practice for a shepherd to use his staff to wrack his sheep over the backs, slam their bodies, or even to hit them at all. The reference to the rod in each of the above verses may allude to guiding our little ones while they are young and rescuing them from danger. Although there may be an occasional need for punishment, wise parents focus on guiding and encouraging the correct behavior in their children, rather than suppressing wrong behavior with physical punishment. Children need attention for survival; if the only way they can gain attention is by misbehaving, then they will misbehave more and more. On the other hand, if correct behaviors are attended to, noticed, and remarked upon, they will demonstrate these behaviors more and more.

The word "discipline" is derived from the same word as "disciple." As Christians, we're taught that when we disciple someone, we teach them, pray with them, read God's Word together, and encourage them as they attempt to lead the Christian life. Physical punishment is not the exclusive meaning of the word "discipline." We can also disciple our children by teaching them, praying with them, reading God's Word together, and encouraging them.

All I'm Created to be

Was there a pattern of discouragement in your childhood? Describe any discouragement you felt. Include phrases used, facial expressions, and mannerisms used by those who discouraged you.

How did you deal with the discouragement?

Set Free

This is an important step for you to take: Think quietly for a few minutes about what you'd like to tell those who discouraged you as a child. Write what you'd like to say to them now:

Prayer: Lord Jesus, you made me special, one of a kind, unique from any other person. Please help me discover that uniqueness and use it to Your glory.

Exercise 5

....

DEALING WITH OUR LIMITATIONS

For all those who exalt themselves will be humbled, and
those who humble themselves will be exalted.
Luke 14:11, NIV

Frankie is a knockout! She has fine auburn hair, porcelain skin, large green eyes, and a lovely figure without even working at it. Growing up, we were more like sisters than cousins. Frankie entered and won several beauty contests—and she deserved to win! She had a personality as lovely as her physical appearance, and I was always delighted to hear of her victories.

This story, however, is not about Frankie but about those of us who're not as fortunate as her. Most of us are considerably less than perfect. As we learn more about who we are, and how and why we've become those people, we may recognize that some imitations are more a part of our genetic makeup than a result of our childhood environment. We've flaws in our physical appearance or we lack some great personality characteristics we see others display. Perhaps, we're not among those fortunate enough to be in the upper percentile of every intelligence test. But if we allow our limitations, rather than our abilities, to dominate our thinking, it can lead us into a trap – almost like reclining on a soft cushion of self-pity, of giving up and dwelling only on our shortcomings.

When limitations, hopelessness, and self-doubt dominate our thoughts, we're tempted to believe we're incapable of serving God in any way. We think we're too flawed to be used in His service. If we spend our time ruminating over our fate: how unfair life has been to us, how badly we were treated, how insignificant and ignored we are, and how dismal the future seems to us, we can miss the blessing imbedded in Jesus' words, "Do not let your hearts be troubled" (John 14:1, NIV). What if, instead of fretting over our limitations, or qualities we lack and how bad life has treated us, we face these limitations courageously? Instead of insisting that God make us perfect, we lay our flawed selves on the altar of sweet sacrifice to God to be used by Him: flaws, warts, and all!

If we stop demanding that God make us like other persons before making ourselves available to Him and to others, we may be surprised by what He will do. I think God knows how much courage it takes to face our weaknesses and still be willing to serve Him. In risking exposure of those weaknesses to the world, there's a special delight that can come from trusting Him and knowing that our successes are attributed to His strength, rather than to our own talents. It really doesn't matter that we lack natural charm, nor that we're imperfect. He has a plan for each of us. Our hope and our value rest on our willingness to trust Him with who we are and letting Him use us in His creative, exciting plans for our lives.

Spiritual Prep: *Jeremiah 29:11-13; Matthew 25:14-30*

All I'm Created to be

What is my best personality trait?

What is my least favorite personality trait?

What are my limitations as I see them?

Whom would I most like to resemble and why?

Set Free

Spend a few quiet moments asking God to show you who He has created you to be and how He can use your personality traits. Write down ways that you think that He can use you in His service:

Prayer: Father, I surrender to You my weaknesses, my limitations, my shortcomings. I ask You to use me to Your glory. Make my attitude a positive one, eager to share Your love by following the path You set out for me.

STEP TWO

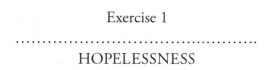

Exercise 1

HOPELESSNESS

For You are my hope; O Lord God, You are my confidence from my youth.
Psalm 71:5, NIV

"I'm bored. I feel so empty and hopeless. There's just nothing I can do to make life better," Brad said as we met in my office to work out a degree plan and course schedule. Brad was not a traditional student. He'd been employed for several years at a variety of jobs, mostly common labor. He felt that all those years had been terribly wasted and that there was nothing he could do to positively change his life. Recognizing Brad's sharp intelligence, the minister of Brad's church had encouraged Brad to take courses at our college, but Brad was certain he wouldn't be able to pass the course requirements nor get a degree.

Brad's mother was a strongly opinionated and outspoken individual. His father was a quiet man until he'd too much to drink. Most of Brad's childhood was spent hiding in his room while his mother and father fought violently. Although he was never physically abused, Brad described the persistent fear that gripped him as a child and still held him prisoner. I was glad that Brad was seeing a professional therapist, and I felt it appropriate that he was taking an antidepressant. I offered an open door to him to come and talk with me any time he'd like, hoping that would give him some additional support.

Brad and I spent many hours talking together. He kept me updated on his progress, both academically and with his therapist. It took Brad three years of college and continued therapy to begin to develop confidence and overcome his sense of helplessness, but his struggle paid off. During those years, Brad became a friend and a caring model to many of the younger students who looked up to him. Brad, along with his sweet family, is now serving as a minister and Christian counselor to individuals from troubled families.

Every life has times when we wonder if anything we do will make a positive change in our lives or our world. Our tasks may seem trivial and we may see no one profoundly touched or changed by coming into contact with us. When there's no visible positive outcomes from our work and no recognition for our efforts, we begin to question, "What value am I, Lord?" We want to hold great revivals, win many souls, build new churches, and not feel like life is passing us by. If early years taught us, like Brad, to be afraid of stepping out, to doubt ourselves and our abilities, then we may be especially vulnerable to feelings of helplessness and hopelessness. If so, it may be wise to talk with a counselor, safe person, or minister.

Remember that with God, all things are possible. Although life may seem barren and unproductive, God will use your efforts. He will take your unique abilities and give you opportunities to express them. He has a plan for your life! Put your trust in Him. Sometimes the greatest work is accomplished by those who walk most humbly, most quietly with Him, without ever being aware of their achievements.

Our lives can become rivers of living water to persons in our paths at school, in the neighborhood, at the office, or sitting next to someone on an airplane. If, in the still moments when we draw closer to God, we allow Him to point out how we can best serve Him, He will bind us more tightly in His arms of love, honor our service, and put a song in our hearts. He will use the abilities He's given us—even if we see no results—if we strive to remain close to Him.

Spiritual Prep: *Psalms 37:7; Isaiah 25:9; 40:31; Hebrews 10:36; James 1:4*

All I'm Created to be

1. Are you afraid of any of the following:
   a. Being a failure
   b. Being rejected
   c. Conflict
   d. Criticism

If you answered "yes" to any of the above, try and write out an explanation of why you are afraid of that particular thing:

2. Have you ever felt numb, hopeless, or empty? If so, describe the times and circumstances when you most felt this way.

Set Free

Prayerfully make a list of the following, allowing God to speak to you as you do so:

1. Things you do well

2. Successes you've had:

Prayer: Lord Jesus, when I feel hopeless and empty, remind me that I'm Your child. Show me how valuable I am in Your eyes and overflow my life with rivers of Your love.

Exercise 2

....

FRUSTRATION

When morning came, there was Leah! So Jacob said to Laban, "What is this you have done to me? I served you for Rachel, didn't I? Why have you deceived me?"
Genesis 29:25, NIV

Every adult encounters frustrating circumstances at some time in their lives. How they handle the frustration depends a lot on the coping mechanisms they've learned as children. One of the ways that unhealthy families function is by creating rigid and negative rules and regulations such as:

- Don't contradict me
- Be seen and not heard
- Don't talk about family matters outside this house
- Don't express strong emotions
- Do as I say (not as you see me do)
- Don't be upset, angry, or cry
- Don't talk back to me
- Don't question me

Being entangled in this stifling web of unspoken and oppressive rules creates frustration which a child often carries into adulthood. Not learning how to cope in a healthy manner with frustrating circumstances often leaves a person without the skills to handle frustration as an adult.

I remember one particularly frustrating day I experienced and didn't handle well. My car refused to start. There it sat, several thousand pounds of useless steel. Grudgingly, I walked to the campus where I taught and, once there, I requested keys to the school's car to reach an urgent dental appointment later that day.

As the afternoon wore on, I caught myself trapped in my office listening to a small group of students who were adamantly expressing anger toward a fellow faculty member. Minutes crept close to my appointment. I rushed out of my office at the last minute to get to the college car, only to find that the keys were not where they were supposed to be. Frantically, I searched for the person responsible for the car. Unable to find him, I telephoned the dentist office to delay my appointment, but couldn't hear the extremely soft voice of the receptionist.

I was totally frustrated. I was upset with the person who misplaced the keys, the students for taking my time to complain about another teacher, the administration for paying a salary too inadequate to repair the car sitting in my driveway at home, and the dental receptionist with the soft voice. I was absorbed by all these minor irritations and blaming everyone and everything for my frustration. Where was all the joy and love that had blessed my heart that very morning as I spent time with God? Furious by this time as well as frustrated and upset, I began walking back home.

Having to walk home was the best thing that could happen to me. It was an early Spring day, the air was only slightly warm, and the day was lovely. The walk gave me the break I needed and cleared my thoughts. Without any other recourse, I calmed down and gained some perspective. I remembered my devotions that morning and found myself talking with God. He responded with the gentle touch of His Holy Spirit and I delighted once more in the beauty of the day.

Review today's Scripture passage at the beginning of this exercise. Frustrating circumstances will pass. Leah was eventually blessed with more children than Rachel. Jacob served Laban for another seven years and went on to become one of the great patriarchs. Perhaps their victory was won because they focused more on the sovereign God than on the temporary thorns in their paths.

Spiritual Prep: *Romans 5:3–5; Colossians 1:11–12; 2 Thessalonians 1:4; Hebrews 12:1–2; James 5:7–11*

All I'm Created to be

1. Things that frustrate me:

2. When I'm frustrated, it feels like:

3. I respond to frustration by:

4. After the frustration passes, I feel:

Set Free

Reflect on the above list of items that frustrate you and rank your reactions to them from 1 to 10, with 1 being completely calm and 10 being the most frustrated you can imagine. Allow yourself to experience the feelings accompanying each situation. Lift these feelings honestly up to God. When you've completed this, quietly ask for and allow God's peace to fill your heart. Once you are calm and aware of His peace, reflect on and write down anything that comes to mind about each of the following as they relate to your feelings of frustration:

1. Cause

2. Prevention

3. Management

4. Healing

Prayer: Father, when frustration threatens to overwhelm me, call me to focus on You. Ease me out of the feelings of frustration with the comfort of Your presence and show me how You want me to respond.

Exercise 3

....

ANXIETY

Commit your way to the Lord; trust in Him and He will do this.
Psalm 37:5, NIV

Anxiety is sometimes described as an "on edge" or "walking on eggshells" feeling. Persons experiencing anxiety often struggle with deeply rooted fears of others' anger, rejection, and abandonment. They may find it difficult to be authentic and spontaneous for fear of being exposed or shamed.

Larry was a tall, good-looking, intelligent young man. When he arrived on campus, he quickly became the center of attention. Female students looked, whispered to friends, giggled, or tried to get his attention when he was nearby. Not only did Larry become our top psychology major academically, but he promised to be a pleasure to have in the classroom. Larry was a serious student and seemed more mature than others his age. Inside and outside the classroom, Larry was cooperative and caring, a kind and gentle Christian witness to those around him.

Larry's seriousness had an edge to it, however. Faculty and students began to realize that Larry demanded an academic perfection of himself that was unhealthy. Always the first at my office door after the most recent exam, he'd want to know his grade immediately. My expressions of assurance that he'd done well (he almost always made the top grade in the class) were not sufficient to relieve his anxiety. "Don't worry!" I'd say, "We both know you did extremely well."

But Larry seemed driven to know that his work met his professors' expectations. I reassured Larry that doing his best was all that was expected of him. Still, he was unable to be at peace until his grade was among the highest in the class. Larry would become upset and depressed if his exam or project didn't receive the top grade. The only time I ever saw Larry become angry and complain that the assignment was unfair, unclear, or impossible was on the rare occasion when his grade was not a perfect score. Eventually, Larry's compulsiveness about his grades began to annoy other students as well as faculty. His anxiety attached itself to any project he did, including job applications, letters to graduate schools, and course papers. Larry's fear of being a social outcast gradually became a self-fulfilling prophecy, and Larry couldn't understand why.

Anxiety often has its roots in persistent attempts to manipulate and control others' opinions of us, especially if we've survived a difficult childhood where we were made to feel ashamed of ourselves. We can't bear to let others see who we think we really are. They might hurt us as we've been hurt in the past, so we try to prevent a recurrence of that hurt by manipulating and controlling what they think. We are never able to control others' perceptions, however, and failure to do so causes us great anxiety. Larry felt that he must always be the best in every task to keep from being rejected by all, otherwise they would know how really worthless he was. His perfectionism was an attempt to prevent others from verifying what his low self-esteem led him to believe about himself.

There are circumstances that merit worry and anxiety, especially if God is left out of the picture. Concern can be healthy if it relates to a specific situation and leads us to think about what we can do to make the situation better. Jesus wept tears at the death of a beloved friend. We would be emotionally shallow if we were never concerned about a loved one who's sick, troubled by failure or financial burdens, or disturbed by unfairness and deception.

Anxiety becomes a problem when it pervades our entire life. If we are gripped by fear of what other people think, it's not an easy matter to surrender our attempts to control their opinions. The anxiety created by relentless attempts to control others' reactions may be such an ingrained pattern of behavior that professional help or guidance by a Christian counselor is needed to break the cycle. It involves some real soul-searching, hard choices, and repeated efforts to let go and let God have control of our circumstances. Talk therapy over a period of time seems to be especially helpful for managing anxiety by promoting insight, self-esteem, and constructive changes in our choices and behaviors.

The anxiety which results from the self-defeating behavior of trying to control others' opinions of us is not God's best will for our lives. He wants us to be governed by a quiet trust and sweet delight in Him. As you work through the following exercises, turn your circumstances and worries over to the Father. Utilize the resources He provides through His word. He'll give you insight, wisdom, and confidence and help you to resolve your anxiety.

Spiritual Prep: *Psalm 37:3; Matthew 6:25–34; Mark 11:22–24; Luke 12:24; 1 Peter 5:7*

All I'm Created to be

1. List and describe three specific situations, people, or things that make you really anxious and nervous:

2. After describing these three things, answer the following questions:
   - Am I 100% sure that _____ will happen?
   - Is _____ really SO important that my whole future depends on it?
   - Does _____'s opinion reflect everyone else's?

Set Free

Read through each of the following types of statements:

1. An anxious thought ("What if I can't do it?" "I will fail." "People are going to laugh at me." "I'm going to go crazy if I can't stop feeling so anxious." "Things are not going to work out." "I'm an idiot.")
2. A coping statement ("This has happened before and I know how to handle it." "My anxiety won't last forever." "All that really matters is that I do my best." "I know that God has the power to help me do what He wants me to do." "If I don't get this job, there will be other opportunities.")
3. A positive statement about yourself ("I can do this." "I'm not a loser because this person dislikes me. No one is liked by everybody!" "I'm not crazy/weak/stupid for having anxiety. Everyone is anxious sometimes.")

Take each of the situations/persons/things you listed and, using the space provided below, write three statements, one statement each in the categories above. Note how you feel after you write the positive statement about yourself.

Situation/person/thing # 1:
Anxious thought:

Coping statement:

Positive statement about myself:

Situation/person/thing # 2:
Anxious thought:

Coping statement:

Positive statement about myself:

<u>Situation/person/thing # 3</u>:
Anxious thought:

Coping statement:

Positive statement about myself:

Prayer: Lord, help me to recognize my anxiety and then put that which triggers it in Your hands completely. Help me to trust You in all circumstances, knowing that You are in sovereign control.

Exercise 4

....

ANGER

The mind governed by the flesh is hostile to God; it does not submit to God's law,
nor can it do so. Those who are in the realm of the flesh cannot please God.
Romans 8:7–8, NIV

Heather was such a pretty name for such an angry person! At the time I knew her, she worked in the administration office at the college where I taught. Heather was angry at the world. Students strongly disliked her. Faculty, other administrators and secretaries avoided her when possible, but Heather never acknowledged any anger. She always made a point of smiling at everyone she offended and often, since she was a minister's wife, ended frustrating encounters with students, faculty, and administrators alike with her practiced response, "God loves you!"

Heather's painful smile failed to mask a troubled, hostile person. She was the only one fooled by the smile. When a student made a valid complaint, Heather's response would inevitably be to deny the validity of the complaint or rationalize her own contributions to the problem. This she would do in a cold but calm voice, and with the forced smile on her face. Yet her eyes betrayed her anger, and her words carried the intent of wounding the complainer. Heather and her husband, who had similar problems in the church where he ministered, took an early retirement right before I moved to a position at another campus. I don't think they ever resolved the anger issues that drove them both to an early retirement.

Anger is an authentic emotional response to appropriate situations. To simply deny its existence is unhealthy. While Scripture often addresses the issue of controlling unruly and inappropriate anger, God's Word also states that there is a place for the expression of authentic anger. "'In your anger do not sin': Do not let the sun go down while you are still angry, and do not give the devil a foothold" (Ephesians 4:26–27, NIV). It's no small accomplishment to be able to recognize, accept and deal with one's anger in a constructive way, especially if we were treated poorly as a child. But learning to express appropriate anger effectively increases our confidence and positive sense of self. We don't want to betray ourselves by denying and avoiding anger at all costs. Nor do we want anger to become a constant, motivating force for our actions. It's an accepted medical fact that chronic anger and deep-seated hostility increase the risk of heart attack, cancer, and stress-related illnesses.

Emotional and physical mistreatment in childhood offers children no liberty to express anger. They carry it like a potential volcano into adulthood where it releases itself in explosive and destructive ways against those who hurt them. Their inability to control and confront, in a positive way, those who cause pain or violate them as adults can lead to chronic, destructive anger. Christians are not exempt from this source of anger. Nor are we exempt from the need for professional help when anger reaches destructive proportions.

If you're struggling with anger, here's a tip that might help you: Try to locate the true source of your anger. Are you still responding to the hurts of childhood? Are you compromising yourself to gain the acceptance you desire? Are your beliefs, values, or trust being violated? Is your competence in question? Recognizing the actual source of our anger can help us evaluate more clearly what currently does or doesn't merit anger.

Even as we struggle to understand the reasons for our anger, our minds can begin to heal. In our daily walk with Him, we can face our anger honestly and ask Him to reveal its cause to us. Then as our eyes are opened, we can choose to release that anger, and the circumstances which trigger it, into His hands. We can set our minds on the joy of His presence in our lives and allow ourselves to drink in His blessings. With God's help and guidance, we can experience victory over chronic anger and nourished resentments.

Spiritual Prep: *Psalm 37:8; Proverbs 14:29; 15:1; Ecclesiastes 7:9; Ephesians 4:31– 32; James 1:19–20*

All I'm Created to be

Think back for a while to your early childhood, and describe a situation which made you really angry:

How did you handle your anger?

Set Free

Anger is not inherently bad. It's a normal emotion like fear, sorrow, happiness, and plays an important role in our lives. Inappropriate anger is anger that becomes your primary emotional response to life and to other people. If this is happening to you, then learning to recognize when you're angry and understanding why you're angry are crucial to doing something about it.

When you're really angry, which of the following symptoms do you show?
_____ breathing faster
_____ sudden explosion
_____sullen, silent treatment
_____yelling, screaming, shouting
_____say things you regret
_____body and hands shake
_____dizziness
_____tension in your jaw, neck muscles
_____knots in your stomach
_____pounding heart
_____sweating
_____angry, red face
_____headaches
_____crying

Do you still get angry if you think of the bad things other people did to you in the past?

Do you wake up at night thinking about those things that upset you?

If someone angers you, do you spend time thinking about putdowns and cutting replies you wish you had made?

Do you wish you could get even with the person who angers you?

Do you usually feel justified in being angry?

How much do you want to do something about your anger?

Are you aware of how God feels about your anger and how you express it?

Do you have hope that, with God's help, you'll be able to do something about your anger?

Prayer: Father God, teach me how to express appropriate anger. Show me the reasons behind my anger when it's not appropriate, and help me to find healing for the source of that anger.

Exercise 5

....

NEGATIVISM

But no human being can tame the tongue. It is a restless evil, full of deadly poison. With the tongue we praise our Lord and Father, and with it we curse human beings, who have been made in God's likeness.
James 3:8–9, NIV

Family traits are often passed down from parents to children. This is beneficial when such traits as nurturing, encouragement, listening skills, cooperative behaviors, etc., are passed on from parents to child. In a dysfunctional family, however, there is a lot of tension, anxiety, negativity, and pessimism. Children sense and are very vulnerable to family attitudes and form patterns of behavior like those of the family or, sometimes, in reaction to family attitudes.

Lindsay recognized in herself the tendency to perpetually criticize and tear down other people, and she was aware of its origin. She desperately wanted to change. I reassured her that she was well on her way to changing the tendency because of her awareness. She not only acknowledged it; she wanted to change! I was certain that her faith in God and willingness to follow His guidance would enable her to make the change she wanted. But because Lindsay was eager to take some immediate steps, I suggested a simple exercise to her. I told her to wear an elastic band around her wrist for a week. Each time she found herself criticizing or gossiping about someone, she was to lightly snap her wrist.

After the week was up, she told me that the exercise helped a lot. However, she also came to realize that she would have to learn new ways of responding to others. With God's guidance and hard work, her efforts paid off. Over the next couple of years, Lindsay became one of the most positive and admired Christian leaders on campus.

Negative people focus on the flaws in situations and in others. Their conversations are mostly about things they dislike. They are cynical and pessimistic. I've seen gossip and criticism disguise themselves in the form of concern and prayer requests. In the same breath that the holy God was called upon, the person for whom prayer was requested was being slandered. Negativity and criticism counteract a positive, productive Christ-like life.   Constant criticism and negativity is an effort to mask low self-esteem—a need to see the weaknesses of others in order to feel good about one's self and one's own personality. As with other emotions and habits, the first step toward changing a destructive thought process is admitting that the problem exists. It takes time and conscious effort to override negative thinking and begin developing a more positive attitude. But with God's help, we have the ability of break free of negative, critical thinking and even rewire our brains to think positively.

Spiritual Prep: *Psalms 34:13–14; 101:5; Proverbs 16:28; Matthew 7:1–5; Galatians 5:14–15*

All I'm Created to be

Sometime today, find and talk with at least three of your friends and/or family. Ask them to describe a time when they felt you were being negative about something or someone else. Take a notepad with you and jot down their responses. Before this day ends, record the responses of your three friends below.

Friend # 1 said I was negative when:

Friend # 2 said I was negative when:

Friend # 3 said I was negative when:

Set Free

Let's work on training our thoughts in a more positive direction. Continue with the following two exercises throughout this week:

1. At the end of each day this week, make a list of three good things that happened that day.
2. At some time during the day, say thank you or express a word of appreciation to someone for their efforts. At the end of the day, record your positive comment below:

DAY 1
1.
2.
3.
Positive comment I made today:

DAY 2

1.

2.

3.

Positive comment I made today:

DAY 3

1.

2.

3.

Positive comment I made today:

DAY 4

1.

2.

3.

Positive comment I made today:

DAY 5

1.

2.

3.

Positive comment I made today:

DAY 6

1.

2.

3.

Positive comment I made today:

DAY 7

1.

2.

3.

Positive comment I made today:

Prayer: Lord, help me to become a more positive person. Teach me to see others as Christ sees them and to encourage the good in them.

Exercise 6

....

ACCEPTING RESPONSIBILITY FOR OUR ATTITUDES

For the Spirit God gave us does not make us timid, but gives us power, love and self-discipline.
2 Timothy 1:7, NIV

Bitterness, anger, hopelessness, negativism, and other destructive emotions can infest anyone's life, but those who've grown up in troubled families are especially vulnerable. If we resort to pretending that these feelings don't exist or blaming others for them, the attitudes often become even more debilitating. Shawn was a bitter person. While she never pretended she was otherwise, she always found a cause or person to blame for her bitterness.

"Isn't that awful about Ellen losing her son without being able to say good-bye to him," Shawn asked, restraining me with this question that was really a statement. I, too, felt deep sadness for Ellen who'd heard secondhand of the death of her grown son.

Before I could express my concern for Ellen, however, Shawn rushed on. "I felt the same way Ellen felt when I heard that Nathan, my brother, had died. Nathan's wife is a real witch."

Shawn continued as her face flushed with anger and her voice became even more vehement. "I just can't forgive her for what she did! Do you know she wouldn't let me see Nathan at all during those last few months? What kind of person would prevent a sister from seeing her brother when he was dying?"

Shawn's face grew even more passionate and disturbed as she exclaimed how Nathan's wife had refused to talk to her after Nathan's death. Scarcely pausing for breath, words tumbled out of her mouth as anger flashed in her eyes. Shawn's struggle with bitterness and anger had existed before Nathan's death; but now, as always, the feelings had something concrete with which to attach themselves. The story of Nathan and his wife had been repeated to many people. The blaming words spilled out like water over a dam threatening to burst from the weight.

I attempted to calm the situation and suggested to Shawn that her bitterness seemed to be causing her a lot of pain. "No, it's not my bitterness that causes pain," she almost screamed. "It's that woman! If I could just tell her to her face what a witch she is, I'd be okay!"

Blaming others for our emotions gets us off the hook by making them responsible for what happens to us. It offers us some measure of relief, but the relief has a high price. The cost is loss of control over our own well-being. When we give up control of ourselves by blaming others, the result is increased anxiety, depression, and a loss of sense of self.

Shawn was making herself ill with her bitterness. As long as she blamed another for that bitterness, rightly or wrongly, she could not get better. The blame game perpetuates malcontent. It gets us nowhere in restoring healthy interpersonal relationships. To continue to take the perspective that someone or something else is to blame will only leave us powerless, resentful, and bitter. When you stop blaming others, you will begin to discover who you really are.

Maturity means taking responsibility for ourselves: our thoughts, our emotions, our actions, and our reactions. This doesn't mean that the situation is our fault or that we caused it, but it does mean that we're taking the responsibility to respond, to take action—to do something.

Granted, assuming responsibility for our actions is easier to talk about than to do. However, we need to do more than just tell ourselves that we're going to accept responsibility (although that's a start in a healthy direction). We need to acknowledge to ourselves that beginning now, with God's help, we'll make it a point to accept responsibility for what we say and do. If we assume responsibility for our lives, our choices, our decisions, this will empower and free us. Our future becomes what we choose to make it. Our ultimate success will depend on us and not on the actions of others.

Spiritual Prep: *Ezekiel 18:20; Matthew 7:3-5, 12:37; Romans 3:19–24; 14:12; Ephesians 4:31–32; Hebrews 12:14–15*

All I'm Created to be

This may be the most crucial part of your pilgrimage, so let's do some real (and perhaps difficult) work here. Dig deeply into your heart and mind, and describe one or more behaviors and/or emotions in your life for which you've blamed others:

Set Free

For just a minute, assume responsibility for these emotions and/or behaviors. How does that make you feel? What behavior changes in your life might you need to make as a result? Ask God for clarity as you seek to answer these questions, and write out any thoughts you have:

Prayer: Father, free my heart from bitterness and blaming, and help me to see the changes You desire me to make in my attitudes.

STEP THREE

The Ashes Of Destructive Relationships

Exercise 1

....

THE MEANING OF LOVE

Then Mary took about a pint of pure nard, an expensive perfume; she poured it on Jesus' feet and wiped his feet with her hair. And the house was filled with the fragrance of the perfume.
John 12:3, NIV

Relationships are complicated! Even more, relationships formed by individuals from troubled families may prove to be extremely difficult to maintain and enjoy. Whether it's friendships, professional relationships, or romantic relationships, these relationships are often characterized by conflict, fighting, and feelings of being misunderstood. If we anticipate the rejection we felt as a child, we may withdraw altogether before a relationship has had a chance to develop. Children from homes with inadequate parenting may not develop the personal characteristics that are needed for a healthy, mature relationship such as self-confidence, trust, self-awareness, and assertiveness.

Workshops or classes on interpersonal skills offered by a local community college, church, family service agency can help. However, even when we've developed the skills and self-acceptance needed for a healthy relationship, there's no guarantee that love will be a story with a happy ending.

What is love? Love isn't one single thing. There's love for our neighbor, love for parents, children, love for our partner, love for our country and love for God. Jesus said, "Whoever has My commands and keeps them is the one who loves Me. The one who loves Me will be loved by my Father, and I, too, will love them and show Myself to them." (John 14:21, NIV) The type of love to which our Lord refers is selfless, unconditional and sacrificial. It's agape, the highest type of love.

Each of us has some understanding of love. We know that, without it, life can seem empty, meaningless, even painful. Although its full meaning may elude us, we sense that love is as necessary as the air we breathe; and obtaining it can become an all-consuming obsession.

Love is a coming-together of two separate but whole people. It's an interdependence, an emotional connectedness between two individuals who have distinct thoughts, feelings, and beliefs. It seeks the growth and expression of the God-given uniqueness of each party. It allows, even rejoices in, the freedom for each person to become all he or she can be, to share openly differing thoughts and feelings about important issues and to pursue avenues of growth that will encourage a more solid sense of "I" as well as "we" within the relationship.

Love means balance. It necessitates an honest understanding of what each is bringing to the relationship, so that neither person silences nor sacrifices his or her own needs in order to meet the needs of the other. It involves clearly defining the roles, responsibilities, and limits of the relationship in a mutually acceptable and tolerable way. To love means becoming vulnerable. It means taking the risk of being honest so that the relationship is founded on reality rather than deception. It means caring enough to reveal differing perspectives in order to facilitate both one's own and the other's growth.

Love means committing ourselves to the beloved, for better or for worse. But commitment is far more than promising undying love. Commitment means keeping promises. It means being consistently there for the other person. It means creating a small island of security for each other. It means that you can be counted on. It means making space in your heart and life for the other, and to always be there no matter how crowded your life becomes.

Love is extravagant. It offers us a taste of heaven as we allow the great, unfathomable love of Christ to permeate our lives and our relationship with our beloved.

Spiritual Prep: *Song of Solomon 8:6; Romans 12:9; 1 Corinthians 13 (the whole chapter);* Galatians 5:14; 1 John 4:12–18

All I'm Created to be

Who was your best friend in elementary school?

Who was your best friend in high school?

Who was/is your worst enemy?

Who was your first crush?

Who is the person with whom you feel most comfortable sharing confidential information with today?

Who are the most precious people in your life today?

Set Free

Think for a moment about what you'd like to tell each of the people who are most precious to you. Write it out below:

Prayer: Father, help me to bring wholeness, balance, honesty, and commitment to each of my relationships and to love others with Christ-like love.

Exercise 2

....

EMOTIONAL TRAPS

Come, all you who are thirsty, come to the waters; and you who have no money,
come, buy and eat! Come, buy wine and milk without money and without cost.
Isaiah 55:1, NIV

An awareness of and respect for boundaries is an important part of any healthy relationship. Boundaries are a measure of our self-esteem and, without them, we can be taken advantage of, put down, and even damaged. People with weak boundaries lack a sense of "self" and are often vulnerable to exploitive situations. In healthy relationships, individuals do not step over each other's limits.

Strong boundaries don't allow individuals to take each other for granted, make fun of, or treat each other badly. Boundaries are "no trespassing" signs. The four general types of boundaries are material, mental, physical, and emotion. These catagories include specifics such as personal space, touching, sexuality, alcohol and substance abuse, finances, what you'll lend and not lend, time and the recognition that your time is valuable. They include values, opinions, beliefs, work, health/self-care, critical remarks, put downs, aggression, saying yes when you mean no, speaking up for yourself, putting others needs before yours, and wrongly taking responsibility for the other person's feelings. Personal boundaries are the limits you decide about how people treat you, how they behave around you, and what they can expect from you.

Laura never had the opportunity to form personal boundaries as a child. Her over-protective mom and controlling father gave her no privacy, no space to develop a sense of self apart from them. Having reached her young adult years, Laura had failed to establish boundaries and develop a definitive, separate sense of self. She continued to look to others, as she had to her parents, for her sense of personal identity. When she first reached beyond her family for a close, caring relationship, she did so unaware that she lacked the boundaries needed to separate her sense of self from others' opinions of her.

In her latest relationship, Laura had become dependent on her new friend, Jerry, to supply her need for esteem and feelings of worth. He became her world. His personality filled the tremendous gaps in her life. She felt whole and able to tackle any problem as long as Jerry was on her side. But if he disapproved of her thoughts or actions, or if she felt the slightest twinge of rejection, she was devastated.

Laura tolerated any criticism, excused any deception, accepted all guilt for any problem. She expended enormous amounts of energy, time, and effort to please Jerry and gain his approval. She pushed away any hurt and anger for fear of losing what little warmth remained. Laura believed his broken promises and lies over and over, and forgave and forgot until her heart turned to stone and she found she could no longer care. She had felt that, somehow, if she could just do enough, she would gain the love and attention from Jerry which validated her as a person of worth.

When she finally realized it was impossible to keep Jerry's love, Laura turned to God. In childlike trust, while the battle she could not win continued to rage, she asked God to help. God's love held her steadfast. Eventually, in His own timing, God made Laura aware of the destructive nature of her relationship with Jerry. God provided her with His peace, and helped her center her life on Him as she tentatively established her own boundaries.

If you're involved in a self-perpetuating cycle of destructive relationships because you lack respect for your own or other people's boundaries, your challenge is twofold. You must first listen to yourself as well as to God—and then make some difficult choices. Listen to your own needs and feelings, and trust what your mind is trying to tell you. It will take time to build a sense of selfhood that tends to its own boundaries and respects the boundaries of others.

Most importantly, listen to Jesus. He is the Living Water. He will satisfy your thirst for selfhood as you allow Him to guide you in setting boundaries. And far more than this: He will provide opportunities to form healthy relationships and transform your soul into a watered garden as you learn to develop intimacies of His choosing.

Spiritual Prep: *Psalms 26:2-4; 36:7; Ecclesiastes 3:1, 8; Romans 8:37–39; Ephesians 2:4–6*

All I'm Created to be

Describe a destructive relationship in your life and why it was destructive:

Describe a relationship which comforted and encouraged you and what you think made it a healthy relationship:

Set Free

What kind of a relationship(s) are you looking for now?

Spend as much time as you need in prayer, asking God to examine your thoughts about the type of relationship(s) you desire—and to clarify what you, as a Christian, need in a relationship. Then, leave the request for that relationship in God's hands.

Prayer: Lord Jesus, I need healthy, intimate relationships based on a solid sense of who I am. I need to respect both my own and others' limits. Help me to recognize and appreciate the boundaries You've shown me that I need to place around my heart and life.

Exercise 3

....

CONFLICT

Leave your gift there in front of the altar. First go and be
reconciled to them; then come and offer your gift.
Matthew 5:24, NIV

Constructive confrontation, although never easy, may be needed if conflict occurs, boundaries are crossed, or harmful choices are being made in our relationships. If you've ever confronted someone, you know that it's not always welcomed. In fact, many times—regardless of how gentle the confrontation—the results can be strong defensiveness or even denial. If you weren't taught as a child how to deal with conflict in a socially acceptable manner, confrontation may be especially difficult for you and easier to just avoid altogether. There will be times, however, when it's important to speak the truth, even when uncomfortable, with a spirit of caring and a desire to help the other person. Meaningful, positive confrontation can promote open communication and lead to positive changes. If done well, confrontation can actually decrease conflict and increase accountability.

Scripture provides several examples of confrontational situations. Genesis 32–33 tells how Jacob needed to confront his brother, Esau. Jacob was at fault, and Esau had the means to demand vindication if he so desired. Jacob needed to be forgiven by the brother from whom he had stolen a birthright. First Samuel 17 tells of a courageous young warrior, David, seeking to confront a legendary hero of the Philistine army who defied all Israel, Goliath. The common factor in both situations was the presence and guidance of God. It was within the strong interweaving of their lives with His will that both men came to their points of confrontation. They knew these were tasks they had to do. Jacob was afraid and admitted his fear. The innocent courage of David admitted no fear. But both men trusted God completely.

Regardless of how I planned and prayed about moments that demanded a confrontation with a contemporary or a student, I, like many others, always dreaded the task. For a long time, I would break down in tears, or feel uncontrollable anger welling up in me whenever I thought about confronting someone. Yet, I realized that confrontation was a necessary part of my work on campus, and I wanted to do it with a Christian attitude.

I eventually found several tools that made confrontation a much more positive and productive experience. First, it's important to make a distinction between the person and the problem. Then clarify the issue in your own mind and mentally phrase it as a shared problem that both of you need to solve cooperatively. State your concerns concisely and invite the person you confront to help you find a solution. Try not to blame, nor voice negative opinions about others. Use the personal pronoun "I" to explain your feelings, rather than the accusatory "you." Let the other person know how you feel and what you want.

Show respect for the other person's thoughts and feelings by finding a point of agreement. As you tell the person why you're hurt or troubled, also let him or her know that you treasure the relationship and want the friendship to be restored. Aggression begets aggression. If you confront in a judgmental, blaming, nagging, complaining manner, you'll build walls and face rejection more often than sympathy and change. Engaging in a cycle in which increasingly hurtful and angry remarks are traded will only result in a complete breakdown of communication.

Most importantly, make certain that your choice to confront another person is based on God's guidance and not on your own anger. Pray about it. Then set out—even if in fear, even if you're uncertain of what you'll say or do—to act on that guidance. With God as your guide, your effort will bring results that are best for you and for the person whom you're confronting.

David slew his Goliath. Jacob found brotherly love. Perhaps you'll stumble, and your efforts will not be well received. Perhaps you'll never be a hero nor find the resolution for which you hoped. But you will have the peace of knowing that you've done God's bidding; and the next time, when God calls you to confront another, you'll be more skilled and your walk with God will be the stronger for it.

Spiritual Prep: *Jeremiah 1:7–9; Acts 6:8–10; 2 Corinthians 5:18–19*

All I'm Created to be

Think back and remember a person or persons in the past whom you've had to confront. Describe below what happened:

Set Free

Picture in your mind someone whom you need to confront now. Lift that person up to God and ask for God's guidance. Then, write out what you feel you need to say to him or to her as you refer to the tips given in the above reading.

Prayer: Lord Jesus, give me the courage to confront when You lead. Teach me to do so without accusation or aggression but in a positive, helpful way.

Exercise 4

....

FRIENDSHIP

Greater love has no one than this, that one lay down his life for his friends.
John 15:13, NASB

Meredith's right side hurt. It was one a.m. and the situation startled me. "What can I do?" I thought. "I'm responsible for all twelve of these students and if Meredith has appendicitis, we need to get her to a hospital fast." But there was no hospital near the mountain retreat where we were staying, and the clinic at the retreat center had already closed.

"I know where a hospital is, and I'll be glad to ride with you there," said Kay. I had met Kay at the bookstore after the evening program. She was the featured singer during the retreat, and she'd come by our cabin later to join my group's late-night devotions. Not only did all of my students immediately take to this warm, friendly Christian singer, but so did I.

Together, Kay and I got Meredith into the car and headed out on the midnight-dark mountain road. Rain poured down furiously as I drove, and I became more and more afraid. Meredith, clutching her side in pain as she sat in the back seat, was crying. Sensing our fear, Kay reached into the back seat and clasped Meredith's hand in hers, as she began to quietly and calmly sing, "Learning to lean, learning to lean, I'm learning to lean on Jesus. ."

Meredith was diagnosed with having a stomach virus and survived the ordeal with nothing more than a case of stomach cramps. Kay and I have since shared many of life's experiences together, and she has taught me much about the love of God. Twenty years later, I'm still blessed with the enduring friendship of this Christian lady.

While it's true that friends do favors for us and are there to help us when we need them, the real reason for friendship involves more than this. Lasting friends share their hearts' longing and find understanding. Lasting friends care unconditionally, so that each feels free to be himself in the other's presence. Lasting friends support and encourage each other.

"There are friends who pretend to be friends, but there is a friend who sticks closer than a brother" (Proverbs 18:24, RSV). A friend is not someone you use to fill your spare time or someone you claim as a friend only when he or she can be of some assistance or advantage to you. Friends are not disposable when you have more interesting social opportunities. Friendships based solely on utility lack the character needed to become enduring relationships.

Lasting friends enjoy our friendship—not because our friendship is a social advantage to them, but simply because they care. Lasting friends are loyal even when it costs them something. They make the effort to stay in touch, nourish the friendship, and remain faithful even when disappointment sets in. Lasting friends interrupt busy schedules to include each other and go the extra mile, if needed, for each other. Lasting friendships are centered on God's love. They provide the opportunity for Him to love and minister to another through us.

Spiritual Prep: *Proverbs 17:17; 18:24; 27:6, 10; John 15:13*

All I'm Created to be

List your friends in order of closeness. Then, beside each name, describe what you most like about each person:

Set Free

If possible, make a point of finding and spending some time today with each of the friends you just listed. Take a notepad and pencil with you. Ask each friend what he she likes about you. Take the time later today to record their answers here:

Prayer: Lord Jesus, help me to be a true friend, to love unconditionally, and to give priority to those whom You bring close to my heart.

Exercise 5

....

CHRIST-LIKE LOVE

*Beloved, let us love one another, for love is from God; and
everyone who loves is born of God and knows God.*
1 John 4:7, NASB

Barbara was one of my roommates in the Peace Corps. We were confident, strong minded young adults and certain we were part of an enlightened generation. We were also skeptical of institutionalized religion and sensitive to any form of hypocritical or superficial expression of love. Barbara and I took a misguided pride in our conclusion that the enveloping love which we heard many Christians discuss and even profess was impossible and pretentious.

After Peace Corps, we went our separate ways. Barbara married and I, having renewed my Christian faith, entered seminary. I continued to struggle with the concept of love, and the reality of it versus the illusion of it, for years. As a maturing adult, I often wondered if I could ever really obey God's command to love others.

It was never an instantaneous transformation for me. It took many years for God to teach my stubborn heart to begin to love as He loves. But the awareness that He was working in my life came one day during a quiet moment at the college where I later taught.

I sat at my desk, despairing over my failure to win the friendship of one of my colleagues, Evelyn. My position required that I work closely with her, but Evelyn resisted any efforts to cooperate and twisted my motives for trying to do so. At a loss as to what to do, I decided to focus on ministering to my students and just leave my relationship with this colleague in God's hands. As the faces and personalities of my students came to mind—handsome, plain, bright, slow, motivated, or not—I realized that my heart was flooded with love for each one of them. I had always cared for my students throughout my teaching career, but never so purely, gently, and completely as I felt now. I knew, at that moment, that my love for my students was and always had been God's gift. I began to see that the love I felt for my students was the same love that I needed to express for my colleague.

Although I wasn't instantly able to love Evelyn, I realized that if I put this relationship in God's hands, He would eventually enable me to love this abrasive colleague. We never became close friends, but the spark of love that God placed in my heart at that moment did indeed grow until I was able to respond to Evelyn with affection like that which I held for my students.

My roommate in the Peace Corps and I were right in our conclusion that it is humanly impossible to love every person we meet. Nonetheless, as I've permitted Christ to work in my life, to shape my thoughts, and to take control of the circumstances of my life, He has taught me to love others as He loves us. Christian, He who is in you is greater than he who is in the world. He who is in you is love. Trust Him. He will teach your heart to love.

Spiritual Prep: *Deuteronomy 10:12–13; Psalm 91:14; Luke 7:47; Romans 8:38–39;
Jude 20–21*

All I'm Created to be

List three people who inspire you. What is inspirational about each person?

Now, think of one or more individuals who are difficult to like. What makes this person(s) difficult to like?

Set Free

Think again about the individuals who are difficult to like. How could you serve as an inspiration to these individuals and learn to reach out to them with God's love?

Prayer: Lord, teach me more about Your love. Overflow my heart with the love that emanates from You, and help me to release that love to those around me.

Exercise 6

....

LOST LOVE

But rejoice inasmuch as you participate in the sufferings of Christ,
so that you may be overjoyed when his glory is revealed.
1 Peter 4:13, NIV

Betty Ann found her father's funeral difficult, but not for the usual reasons. Her father and mother had been emotionally estranged most of Betty Ann's life with a lot of highs and lows in their marriage. Her dad was an alcoholic, and more often than not he followed a violent and self-destructive path despite the fact that he'd become a Christian earlier in life. Betty Ann told me many things that her father did to make his family ashamed of him, but Betty Ann suspected that her dad's actions shamed him even more than they did the family.

Betty Ann believed that if, in her father's youth, his own childhood circumstances had been healthier, her father's personality would have bloomed and become quite remarkable. Before his addiction took over his life, her father had been a kind, Christian man. One thing Betty Ann recalled from her preschool years was how gentle her father was and how he showed remarkable sensitivity to children and animals. This, Betty Ann said, forever left its imprint on her own life. But her father's gentleness turned to apathy and his kindness was destroyed by increasingly frequent alcohol binges. By the time Betty Ann entered her early school years, her father's love for God and for his family had become marred by depression and anger. Betty Ann's father left home when she was a teenager, but he returned and reconciled with her mother after Betty Ann's graduation from college. He remained free of alcohol from that point on and attended church until his death a few years later.

At her dad's funeral, Betty Ann felt the shock and numbness of being severed from her father, but not the feelings which normally accompany mourning. There were no tears of loss, few regrets. The emotions which the termination of her father's troubled life brought were too tumultuous for Betty Ann to handle as a young woman. She kept all feelings at bay until years later, when nightmares and depression threatened to overwhelm her. Through counseling, Betty Ann was able to turn and confront the unresolved horror, fears, and anguish of this monster, death. In doing so, Betty Ann glimpsed the peace and beauty that accompany the transition from earth to eternity of a soul owned by Christ. "Where, O death, is your victory? Where O death, is your sting?" (1 Corinthians 15:55, NIV).

Perhaps you've lost some people you've loved but who've also hurt you. If they accepted Christ, it may make it even more difficult for you to understand how they lived the way they did—and their death left only unresolved mourning. But one day you will meet them again, and this time you'll understand. Your questions will be answered, and you will see them as Christ meant them to be.

Betty Ann believes now, in heaven, her father has finally begun to walk, with his shoulders back and his head held high, in the direction that Christ beckons him to go. She knows that some day she will meet her father on that path and will find her dad a transformed man with the beauty of the heavenly Father in his face. Betty Ann has the assurance that she will experience the exquisite joy of sharing all eternity not only with her heavenly Father but also with the Daddy that life failed to provide.

Spiritual Prep: *John 5:24; 16:20; Romans 5:1–5; 6:9, 23; 8:28, 1 Corinthians 15:54–57*

All I'm Created to be

How did your family handle grief during your childhood? Did they allow you to talk about your feelings of grief?

Whom have you loved and lost, either through death or through a broken relationship?

How did you deal with that loss or losses?

Set Free

Think about and list one thing in each category which helps you deal with loss and sadness:

Music:

Books:

Places:

Pets:

People:

Scripture verse(s) (write it/them out):

Prayer: Lord Jesus, I thank You for dying on the cross for me. Because You did, I will once again be reunited and live in perfect relationship with those whom I love in heaven where You've finally made them whole.

STEP FOUR

Ashes When We Go Astray

Exercise 1

....

NEUROSIS

Anyone who listens to the word but does not do what it says is like someone who looks at his face in a mirror and, after looking at himself, goes away and immediately forgets what he looks like.
James 1:23–24, NIV

Although the word "neurosis" has long been replaced by more descriptive terms in the <u>American Diagnostic and Statistical Manual of Mental Disorders</u>, I continue to be asked, "Is sin caused by neurosis?" I've often thought about the relationship between the concept of sin and the concept of maladaptive or neurotic behavior. Unhealthy personality tendencies are sometimes related to a biological predisposition, a chemical imbalance, or a complex combination of both. More often, however, they're the results of early learning experiences. We do not choose these tendencies, nor is anyone totally free from maladaptive behaviors. None of us are perfect.

Addictive personalities are frequently the children of addictive personalities. Compulsive behavior in children may follow the pattern of compulsive behavior demonstrated by the parents. Abused children sometimes become abusive parents. We may have learned to greatly exaggerate truths, to become unreasonably jealous, or to wallow in and waste away our lives in remorseful and negative thinking. We may consciously deceive others, use others to get our way, or feel we should always be the center of attention. We may recognize that we are almost always anxious, angry, or sad. We might see in ourselves tendencies to gossip and malign others, to seek sexual objects of an unhealthy nature, or to take advantage of the trust and honesty of others.

However, we don't have to perpetuate these patterns of behavior. That is a matter of choice. Neither learning, genetics, nor any combination of the two necessitate a lifetime pattern of behavior. There may be a biological predisposition toward addictive behaviors, for example, but the choice must first be made to indulge in the thing to which one becomes addicted. Even after the addiction develops, each time we indulge involves some degree of choice.

In every life, there comes a day of awareness. We recognize in ourselves those tendencies, those predispositions, those inclinations to behave in ways detrimental to our own well-being or to the well-being of those around us. When we become aware of these tendencies, then we consciously choose whether to act upon and indulge our unhealthy appetites, or to make the effort to change that tendency.

It's at this point that we may face the most painful, difficult choice we'll ever have to make. At the point of awareness, the behavior we choose becomes our responsibility. Madaptive behavior tendencies, in general, reflect the inherent, imperfect, sinful nature of man. I do not believe that God holds us personally responsible for our tendencies toward neurotic behaviors. I do believe, however, that when we become aware of our specific tendencies—and face the choice of either perpetuating them or doing something about them—that this is where our own personal sin begins or ends. It's at this point that God holds us personally responsible.

Accept that Jesus' death on the cross covers all confessed sin—original sin, which is part of our imperfect nature; and personal sin, which results from our own choices. It may take time, effort, and repeated failures to change. There might be a need to seek a wise counselor, support group, or a good friend through whom God can help us see our options more clearly. Surrender to God that which leads you to be less the new creation that He intends you to be, and He will help you make the right choices. He will send legions of angels to your side. The cycle can be broken.

Spiritual Prep: *Deuteronomy 30:19–20, Joshua 24:15; 1 Kings 18:21; Psalm 119:30; Luke 10:41–42*

All I'm Created to be

Describe a low point in your life, when you recognized you had an internal obstacle to living the Christian life:

Describe some steps you've taken, or plan to take, to overcome that obstacle:

Set Free

As you experience victories (no matter how small) over that internal obstacle, record those victories here. Continue keeping this record even after you finish all of the exercises in this book.

Prayer: Father, as I recognize those things in my life which can be changed, guide me and give me strength to make the right choices.

Exercise 2

·····································

RECOGNIZING SIN

Those who cleanse themselves from the latter will be instruments for special purposes,
made holy, useful to the Master and prepared to do any good work.
2 Timothy 2:21, NIV

Kevin came to me, so distraught by his recent failure in the face of a particularly powerful temptation that he was ready to give up his plans to enter the ministry. He was a talented and intelligent, but lonely, young man with only a small group of friends. In a desire to be accepted by the group, he had done something which he knew was not in God's will for his life. Kevin had tried to hide his mistake from his teachers and mentors and rationalize it to himself, but the awareness of it continued to haunt him. Kevin seemed devastated now by this failure, and intensely felt that God expected better of him.

"I've never met a sinless person," I assured Kevin, and pointed that his distress showed how deeply he loved God and was evidence of the Holy Spirit working in his life. He acknowledged this with relief, and we went on to talk about his desperate need for acceptance by his friends and how this need might deflect him from his call to the ministry. We had several talk-sessions about Kevin's feelings of loneliness and, before graduation, Kevin entered counseling to help him resolve these feelings.

By grappling with his own loneliness and shyness, Kevin grew stronger in his sense of self and more confident in his own decisions. As he gained self-assurance, Kevin chose to remain true to His commitment to God and pursue his goal to become a minister. After graduation, Kevin entered seminary and in the last communication between us, Kevin was serving as the music and youth minister in a small church as he and his sweet wife were expecting a new addition to their family.

We cannot fully grasp the meaning of being delivered from sin until we first recognize the horrible nature of sin that is in us. This realization comes for every individual in unique ways and does not necessitate a firsthand taste of the depravity of which we're capable. For some to realize this, however, God permits the potential for sin to become a reality. Whether we experience it firsthand or not, when we remain blind to the obvious horror of sin we can only mouth, without substance, an appreciation for the purpose of Christ's death on the cross.

Denial, repression, and rationalization are all methods by which we shade our perceptions of our sin. It would be so much easier to pretend that we haven't sinned and to deny the reality of it both to ourselves and to God. We might try to repress sins from our memory without seeking His forgiveness. Frequently we rationalize our wrong choices by making excuses for them, blaming the other person, or claiming it couldn't have been otherwise.

In some manner, all of us must come to grips with the ugliness of our old nature without Christ. Once we're aware of sin, and suffer the dismay of knowing about that which we're capable, we become responsible for our actions. Attempting to hide our choices and cling to what we know to be sinful will only create personal misery, regardless of how much we feel we must have the secret thing. God, the Author of all truth, knows (as surely as any psychologist) that hiding reality from ourselves doesn't dissipate it. Instead, hidden sins ferment and call out for recognition and rectification.

When we experience the nagging guilt associated with sin, at least then we know that we have evidence of the Holy Spirit working in our lives. With His guidance, we can learn to distinguish between the deception of sin and the truth of God. If we allow this insight to create in us a hunger for more righteousness, a desire to be more like Him, and an inclination to sin less, then we are on the path toward assuming the new nature which is His gift to us. The path will not be easy. It will always be fraught with temptations. But Jesus will be there, picking us up when we fail, forgiving us, and pointing to a way free of sin. He will meet our needs abundantly.

Spiritual Prep: *Genesis 4:6–7; 2 Samuel 12:12–13; 1 Kings 8:46–50; Psalm 32:5; Romans 3:23; 1 John 1:5–10*

All I'm Created to be

Because of the importance of this step, this is being combined with the "Set Free" section. On the following page, you'll find the shape of a cross. Take a few minutes and think about any choices you've made which have been destructive to you—choices that you're now aware are outside the will of God. Using a pencil with a good eraser, lightly write—in code if you wish—each of these choices on the cross. As you write of each instance, lift up that choice in prayer to God and ask for His forgiveness. He will forgive you. Over the next few days, continue to pray about these choices, and when you're aware of God's forgiveness, erase each of those choices.

Exercise 3

....

THE WORST SIN OF ALL

Do not merely listen to the word, and so deceive yourselves. Do what it says.
James 1:22, NIV

What's the worst thing you've ever done? Even though you may feel God's forgiveness for most of the sins in your life, does He seem to turn His face when you ask forgiveness for this particular one? Do you feel like you're leading a double life—that if anyone knew what an awful thing you'd done, they'd laugh in the face of your Christian witness?

At some point in our lives, we may come to feel that we've committed a sin so horrible that even God can't forgive us. What we've done is more grotesque than we ever dreamed ourselves capable of doing. Yes, we've asked forgiveness, but perhaps we haven't been sincere enough in confessing the sin, or we just haven't used the right words! And because we think we cannot be forgiven, it becomes more and more difficult, consciously or unconsciously, to forgive others of any sins they commit against us. The words of Matthew 6:12, "And forgive us our debts, as we also have forgiven our debtors," strike us as a condemnation rather than a blessing since we're unable to feel His forgiveness

Christian, take heart, and do not compare God's forgiveness to the human capacity to forgive. His forgiveness is like an infinite ocean which can remove and wash away all human sin, no matter how awful. In recognizing your sin and your own capacity to commit it, you've already taken a great step. Christ's death on the cross was not in vain. His forgiveness runs deeper than any pit into which your choices and behaviors can plunge you. He asks only that you return to him, acknowledge your sin, and ask His forgiveness.

The greatest tragedy for a Christian is not the sin, although all sin is offensive to God. The greatest tragedy in life is the failure to admit sin and seek forgiveness, to pretend it doesn't exist, to attempt to justify it. Some folks even try to justify their sin on partial spiritual truths. We mistreat our children in the name of "biblical" discipline; we intimidate our spouse and expect "scriptural" submissiveness; we oppress those with less strength and demand that they show "servant" obedience; we manipulate and deceive those with whom we live and expect "Christian" cooperation. We point our fingers at those who choose more obvious lifestyles of sin and start crusades against them, while ignoring our own sinful nature.

Once, however, we make the choice to face our own personal sin, we're on the right track. Although we're often overwhelmed by the havoc sin has wreaked, it's never too late. It takes courage, openness, vulnerability, and sensitivity to admit the sin and make the choice to change. Oh, how His angels must rejoice when we face and acknowledge our sin, no matter how awful it may seem to us. Once our sin is acknowledged, confessed, and forgiven, it is no longer impossible to forgive others. We are able to draw from the great reservoir of His forgiveness and cleansing in our own lives.

Claim the forgiveness provided for you when Christ died on the cross, and ask God to free your mind from the suggestion that your sin is somehow unforgivable. Reject the image that God turns His face from you. Accept His perfect love and the new beginning He gives. A doer of the word sees his or her face in the clear reality of God's truth, and in that insight, chooses to turn from the sin. And "they will be blessed in what they do" (James 1:25). Claim the blessing and turn to look, freed from sin, fully into the face of a loving God.

Spiritual Prep: *Psalm 90:8; Proverbs 28:13; Isaiah 1:18–20; Jeremiah 33:8; Acts 13:38–39; Hebrews 10:17*

All I'm Created to be

Describe an instance where you forgave someone for a sin they committed against you:

Describe a situation where someone forgave a sin which you committed against them:

Set Free

On the cross from the previous exercise, write (again, in pencil) a description of the sin that you find the hardest to forgive in your life. Take a few moments and confess this sin to Christ. Ask His forgiveness, wait a few moments in silent prayer, and then erase the sin. If you find yourself returning to this sin (no matter how many times), again write it on the cross, asking Him to forgive you and to give you strength to turn from that sin. Once you're aware of His forgiveness, erase it again as well.

Exercise 4

....

FORGIVENESS

The steadfast love of the LORD never ceases, his mercies never come to
an end; they are new every morning; great is thy faithfulness.
Lamentations 3:22–23, RSV

If God loved only sinless saints, we would all be left out in the cold; but He loves sin stained persons too. God so loved sinners—you and I—that He sent His Son to take our punishment by suffering and dying on the cross for us. Immediately, when we recognize this fact and accept as our personal redemption His death on the cross for us, we are forgiven.

Seeking forgiveness of sin is not an easy task. It can include a lot of anguish. On the other hand, confession and seeking forgiveness promote health of both mind and body. Only when we seek God's forgiveness can our minds and hearts be cleansed. We don't need to allow our failures to drag us down into despair and incapacitate our efforts to serve Him. There's no need to feel that we're doomed to suffer miserable circumstances for each sin we commit. As quickly as we admit our sin and ask His forgiveness, we're forgiven.

Don't be harder on yourself than the Lord is! You can't pay God back for what you did wrong. Jesus has already done that. Despair and guilt and unhappiness are not the fulfillment of the promises of His Word. If we're not bent on punishing ourselves ten times over for every sin we commit, then a life of service to Him can produce a joy and a confidence that nothing else offers. We'll never achieve perfection in this life, nor will we escape the suffering that we bring on ourselves. But if God lives in our hearts, we can meet every circumstance and overcome every sin with incorruptible confidence, because we belong to Him.

Keep asking God to change you to become more like Jesus every day. As your day stretches on, remember to keep a short account with your Heavenly Father. Immediately confess your sins and seek His forgiveness. Then a big, long list never needs to build up. It would be great to meet up with another Christian with whom you can trust to be open and pray about any changes your life might need.

Remind yourself that you are not alone. When you turn back to God in repentance, God rejoices and will forgive you completely. When we awaken in the morning, His mercies are fresh with us! When we become busily involved in our day, His care remains over us. As we retire in the evening, He is still minding us, calling us to seek His companionship, His forgiveness. Remember, it is the love of God for sin-stained persons that is creating tomorrow's saints.

Spiritual Prep: *1 Corinthians 6:11; 2 Corinthians 5:21; Colossians 1:21–23; 1 John 1:9*

All I'm Created to be

Think for a moment about that sin in your life for which you can't feel forgiven. Now, close your eyes and imagine a rope attaching you that sin. Take a deep breath and see that rope being cut by the hands of Christ. Visualize you and the sin gently floating apart releasing the tie between you and the sin. Describe the relief which you feel after being released:

Thank God for releasing you from that sin.

Set Free

Ask God for guidance as you think about how you will live free of the sin you visualized above. Describe how you can continue to put this into practice:

Prayer: Lord Jesus, how wonderful to know that every morning brings a fresh, new supply of Your mercies and Your forgiveness. Thank you for forgiving me.

STEP FIVE

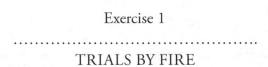

Ashes After Life's Blows

Exercise 1

....

TRIALS BY FIRE

I will restore the fortunes of my people Israel, and they shall rebuild the
ruined cities and inhabit them; they shall plant vineyards and drink
their wine, and they shall make gardens and eat their fruit.
Amos 9:14, RSV

"We're concerned that, with your hearing loss, you won't be able to learn the language of another country," Dr. Wolf, the Medical Director of the Foreign Mission Board, said. I became defensive. I had easily made it into the Peace Corps a few years before, and that was a more strenuous evaluation process! Why shouldn't I just as easily make it through a foreign mission appointment?

"But I learned the language in the Philippines," I replied.

"Did you become fluent in Filipino?" he asked.

"Well, no," I responded, "but that's just because I don't learn languages easily."

"You have difficulty learning because you're unable to hear the subtleties of the language when it's spoken," he said. "Besides, there's something else."

"What?" I began to be alarmed.

"You have a heart murmur," he replied. "It's fairly common, but we did lose a missionary with a similar heart murmur a few years ago."

I was young and enthusiastic, and I felt I knew without a shadow of a doubt that I was to be a foreign missionary. Now the lifelong dream crumbled around my feet, and I faced the first real trial of faith in my young life.

Shadrach, Meshach, and Abednego, in the book of Daniel, experienced a literal trial of faith by fire when they refused to heed the call to worship false gods. Although perhaps not as literally, we as Christians will experience many trials of faith during our lifetimes. The world will beckon us, and our beliefs will be tested.

As new Christians, we determined to yield our lives to God believing—as Shadrach, Meshach, and Abednego did—that we would be true, even when it meant suffering. Then when things didn't go the way we planned and we actually experienced failure, we questioned. "Why did this happen to me, Lord? Have You forgotten me? Do You really care?" We may have cast ourselves on Him, expecting God to remove us from the fire and clear the obstacles in our path. If He didn't, if the path remained blocked, we began to doubt and wonder if God really cared about us.

God doesn't promise us that the Christian life will be free from trials. Quite the opposite: "Beloved, think it not strange concerning the fiery trial which is to try you, as though some strange thing happened unto you: But rejoice, inasmuch as ye are partakers of Christ's sufferings; that, when his glory shall be revealed, ye may be glad also with exceeding joy" (1 Peter 4:12-13, NIV). When you are faced with a trial, stay close to God's word, to the fellowship you find in your church. Don't distance yourself from the tugging on your heart by the Holy Spirit. Pray constantly. As you remain faithful, you will be spiritually strengthened and your faith refined. Like fire transforms iron into steel, in a Christian's life, fiery trials reveal and develop character, prove the genuineness of your faith and validate God's promises that "all things work together for good to them that love God, to them who are called according to His purpose" (Romans 8:28, NIV).

Shadrach, Meshach, and Abednego walked from the furnace untouched by the flames of death. The only thing that burned was the cords that bound them. Christian, hang on. You, too, will eventually walk triumphantly from the valley of suffering and stand resurrected in the newness of your life in Christ. And you will know more of Him, more of yourself, and more of the direction He wants for your life, for having walked through the flames.

Spiritual Prep: *Psalm 121:1–4; Zephaniah 3:17; John 16:33; 2 Corinthians 1:5; 1 Peter 1:6–7*

All I'm Created to be

Describe three instances where you experienced a trial by fire. Where do you think God was, in each of those trials?

Set Free

If you're in the midst of a trial by fire and have yet to escape, think how you might be victorious. Pray about this and allow God to help you find your answers. Write your prayer below.

Prayer: Father God, make Your presence known to me when I go through trials of my faith. Give me strength, and show me how to respond so that Your will is done.

Exercise 2

....

PERSECUTION

They will have no fear of bad news; their hearts are steadfast, trusting in the Lord.
Psalm 112:7, NIV

While serving as a campus minister early in my career, I encountered a professor of psychology, a charming man but one who expressed a strong distaste for Christians and Christianity. Dr. Manley attacked Christian beliefs and called them the source of wars as well as the cause of most of the world's ills. One of his favorite illustrations was the story of a misguided mother he'd known who refused to let her terminally ill son be operated on because she believed the child could be healed by faith. The son later died. Dr. Manley told this story repeatedly, as well as one about a father who perversely claimed, as his Christian right, the submissive acceptance by his daughter of his sexual overtures.

How tragic that these examples exist and exist in abundance among both Christians and non-Christians. But Dr. Manley, wanting to find the cause for the pain with which he daily counseled, placed all the blame squarely on the shoulders of Christianity. Christian beliefs, as he perceived them, were distorted and sick. Dr. Manley felt it was his duty to eradicate any such beliefs from the minds of his students and, in doing so, launched a concerted attack on the Christian faith.

Often the persecution to which Christians are subjected by the world is a very subtle, undercutting pressure, such as that experienced by Christian students in Dr. Manley's classes. The persecution takes the form of a slight putdown, a barely perceptible smirk, or a joke at the Christian's expense. It ostracizes, intimidates, and ignores. From the classroom to the military, Christianity is under assault in our world today. The incidents of persecution are relentless and worsening. Around the world millions of Christians are harassed, slandered, discriminated against by the media and in the workplace, sometimes arrested, imprisoned, beaten, or even killed.

Even as Christians, we sometimes persecute each other. We fight among ourselves, spread rumors, and exclude those who do not believe exactly like we do—or, even worse, we judge them to be unchristian without even knowing their hearts. We deny others places of service based on race, gender, or social standing. When that happens, if we're the ones being victimized by someone claiming to be a Christian, the persecution seems even more difficult to bear.

If you are a victim of persecution, draw close to the heart of Christ. Instead of plotting revenge on your tormentors, seek God's comfort. Trust Him to take care of all of your circumstances. He will calm and strengthen you, and give peace to your heart. He will show you how to deal with the persecution. Rest in His peace, without seeking retaliation and know that God is in control—even in the midst of persecution.

Spiritual Prep: *Psalms 7:1–2, Matthew 5:10, John 15:20–21, 1 Corinthians 4:12–13, 1 Peter 4:14–19, Romans 12:19–20*

All I'm Created to be

List and describe a persecution you've had to endure:

Set Free

Think about the above instance of persecution. Describe how it might (or did) strengthen your walk with God.

Prayer: Father, give me the strength and peace of mind I need to endure persecution from others without retaliation. Above all, Lord Jesus, show me if I'm the persecutor—and if I am, forgive me.

Exercise 3

....

WHEN GOD IS SILENT

When you pass through the waters, I will be with you; and when you pass
through the rivers, they will not sweep over you. When you walk through the
fire, you will not be burned; the flames will not set you ablaze.
Isaiah 43:2, NIV

It was an early Sunday evening. As I sat in a pew of an almost empty church waiting for the program to begin, the late afternoon sun crept soft and warm through the stained glass windows, dumping its golden rays in my lap. The program that evening was a film which told a story of a young boy who was dying of cancer.

The boy's mother, to take his mind off of his suffering, told him to listen for the bells of heaven which Jesus would ring for her child when it was time to join Him in heaven. When the end came and the small boy was in intense pain, the medical attendants were baffled by his smiles and puzzled by his frequent references to the bells. Later they asked the mother about this. She explained that her child had only heard the bells of heaven welcoming him home.

There are times when all of us will face physical or emotional events that trigger a despair which seems unbearable. On these occasions, we may feel completely alone. It might seem like there's no one with whom we can share our sorrow. We can't even reach the bottom of our hurt, but we sense its depth and it frightens us. Our cries to God may seem to fall cold at our feet; and at those times we may sense in ourselves the capacity to grow bitter and angry and turn away from God. "Where are You, Lord, when I can't see Your face?" we ask. "Why do You remain silent when I try so hard to hear you?" In these times, it may be helpful to reach out to a pastor, Sunday school teacher, or spiritual leader who will be supportive and understanding. Don't hesitate to seek out such a person who is caring and sympathetic to your pain.

God's silence can be an opportunity for growth and a deeper understanding of Him. Sometimes His silence is actually His answer. He trusts you to keep the faith while He prepares an even bigger revelation of Himself or brings you to a fulfillment of His purposes for your life. God allowed silence for three days before raising Lazarus.

Is He allowing a period of silence in your life for a reason? Is there an answer to be found in His silence? Remember, His is a still, small voice and we may need to listen closely to hear His voice in the silence.

As I watched the film that Sunday evening, I remembered how God's bells had rung for me at difficult times. When problems loom too large for you to solve, and all you feel from God is silence, stop a moment. Listen. There may be bells from heaven for you also.

Spiritual Prep: *Psalms 28:1–2; Psalms 50:3; Matthew 5:4; 2 Thessalonians 2:15–17*

All I'm Created to be

Describe a problem in your life, current or from childhood, which threatens (or threatened) to overwhelm you:

Set Free

Take a few minutes and lift the above situation (especially if it's a current one) up in prayer to God. Wait and listen silently for His comfort and guidance. If you feel that He's given specific guidance to you during your prayer time, describe it below:

Prayer: Father, when I'm in despair, help me to stop and listen for the music of heaven's bells.

Exercise 4

....

COURAGE TO CONTINUE

Therefore, my dear brothers and sisters, stand firm. Let nothing move you. Always give yourselves fully to the work of the Lord, because you know that your labor in the Lord is not in vain.
1 Corinthians 15:58, NIV

George had just accepted his first teaching position! His new department chair, Allen, seemed to be a dynamic Christian—so full of life that George felt they would make a marvelous ministry team. He thought working for Allen would be a joy and a privilege. A whirlwind of unpacking, preparing materials for rapidly approaching classes, and helping his new wife settle into a temporary apartment all accompanied his move to this place. A small house, more like a little cottage, with ample room for a couple, caught George's eye. It was owned by the college and he could purchase it, if he would do the needed repairs, at a very reasonable price. Several of his colleagues and some of his ministerial students offered to help him do the painting, refinishing, and carpentry needed to make the house livable.

Being reassured by his co-teachers that the cottage was available, he inquired in our college's business office about the procedure involved. Sadly, he learned that the business manager with whom he'd have to deal didn't really want the house sold. George found himself repeatedly blocked, delayed, and manipulated. The manager would fail to keep appointments, allow deadlines with lawyers to pass, and scold George for inquiring into the things that needed to be done. What a way to begin his life in this new location!

But that was only the beginning. Gradually, George's frustration reached an emotional peak and he confided in Allen about the problems he was having. Allen's reaction was cold and unsympathetic. The business manager and Allen had professional ties, and Allen didn't wish to offend this nor any administrator.

George eventually was able to purchase and move into the small house and settle into his new teaching position. He was a remarkable teacher, but as his reputation grew more positive among his students, the relationship between him and Allen became brittle. George became the victim of manipulation and deception by Allen and the business manager. Even though Allen encouraged differing opinions, if George disagreed with him, however gently, his views were deemed unacceptable. George was given poor evaluations by Allen and left out of crucial departmental meetings. He was overlooked for departmental luncheons and holiday gatherings. Although I taught in a different department, I was grateful but surprised when this enthusiastic young professor accepted a second year's contract at our school.

Eventually, Allen and the business manager moved on to a different school while George remained with us. A few years later, George and I were talking about his early rough years at our college, and I asked him how he endured all that had happened. George told me that it was actually one of the most spiritually strengthening times of his life. During, and because of, the continual conflicts he began to see far better what it meant to walk alone with God. He grasped and cherished the belief that in God's eyes, his work wasn't in vain. During the days, weeks, and months spent in these circumstances, George took refuge in God's strength and love as he poured out desperate prayers that God would keep him safe and secure.

A Christian is not immune to gossip and slander! In spite of our best intentions, our efforts will sometimes be misunderstood, ignored, or even deliberately misrepresented. Instead of praise and recognition, we may encounter hostility, jealousy, and petty schemes to undermine what we do. During these times, the real test is whether or not we can remain steadfast in our faith and receptive to the Holy Spirit. George didn't feel that he always lived up to that test, but he kept trying to walk with, talk to, and listen to God. Eventually, he was able to see how God worked through his circumstances. Through all situations, no matter how difficult, cling to God. He will guide your steps as you labor to serve Him.

Spiritual Prep: *Psalms 18:31–33; 27:1; 46:1-3; 91:11–12, Isaiah 26:3–4; Galatians 6:9; 2 Timothy 1:12*

All I'm Created to be

Describe an instance when your actions were misinterpreted or misunderstood. Who were the person(s) involved? How did it make you feel?

Set Free

Take a few minutes, now, and lift those persons involved up to the Lord, asking Him to help you forgive them and to show you how to respond to them now. If any specific thoughts come to mind, write them down.

Prayer: Lord, when I'm doing Your will, help me to persevere. Keep my eyes on You, not on what others say about me. Give me a courageous, forgiving heart as I try to follow Your path.

Exercise 5

....

VICTOR, NOT VICTIM

He tends his flock like a shepherd: He gathers the lambs in his arms and
carries them close to his heart; he gently leads those that have young.
Isaiah 40:11, NIV

The mosquitoes were eating me alive, leaving red, angry bites that made me look like I had the measles. The situation was made even more unbearable by the heat. With no electricity, no fan, and no air-conditioning, my body cooled itself by sweating—and the perspiration only made the itching more ferocious.

In the dry, hot Filipino town, there was no glass for windows nor window screens available. The rough houses were built with large gaps for windows so that the residents could catch any outside breeze. The other Peace Corps volunteers and I put up screening sent from headquarters, choosing to lose a little breeze rather than deal with insects. Still, we shared our living quarters with many of these insects, and they were in abundance: spiders, roaches, mosquitoes, as well as small lizards.

In addition to being plagued by insects, our efforts to keep a budget were a complete failure. The Peace Corps gave each volunteer an allowance in Filipino currency which matched the income of a native Filipino teacher. My roommate, Sandy, and I'd not been able to make it through a single month on our allowance since arriving in the Philippines. The last week of the month was typical, and we were hungry. While discussing what we could do this month, the wife of a missionary stationed in our small town knocked on our screen door and invited us for the evening meal. This became a repeated pattern as other friends would invite us to meals or drop off fresh fruit or produce which sustained us through many an end-of-the-month small hunger crisis.

As I look back, I realize that I matured more during that period of having to survive the difficult monthly budget problems than at any earlier time in life. Uncertain circumstances taught me to look to God for strength. Sandy and I still tried to solve our budget problems ourselves, but I came to intensely value the moment-by-moment guidance from God. I learned to rest my anxieties on Him believing—although perhaps not feeling it at the moment—that He would take care of me. These difficult times, more than anything else, taught me to walk by faith.

It's surprising how hardships can teach us faith and how, through troubling times, we can start to grasp the deep truth that He is ever present with us. The sweetest solace that can be known is the touch of God's hand in the midst of difficult, even terrible, circumstances. When we are so weighed down that we're unable to take a step in any direction, He carries us, sometimes without our knowing it, in His bosom like a shepherd gathering His lambs.

Christian, if only we could see as God sees, perhaps we would recognize the potential for growth that adversity provides. Just as Christ won the victory over suffering on the cross, so can we, through our faith in Him, become victors over suffering rather than victims.

Spiritual Prep: *Psalms 27:5; Romans 5:3-5; 8:17; 1 Peter 3:14–17; 5:10*

All I'm Created to be

Write about a time when you experienced victory over suffering, and describe how you grew from that experience:

Set Free

Is there a miracle that you'd like to see performed in your life? If so, describe it below. Then, lift it up to God in prayer, expecting Him to answer.

SECTION TWO

Rising From The Ashes

STEP SIX

The Phoenix Rises

Exercise 1

....

FAITH INTERNALIZED

"But the righteous will live by his faith."
Habakkuk 2:4, NASB

"I know what I believe!" Malcolm exclaimed, hurt by Rev. Martin's accusations. Malcolm was applying for work on the mission field, but his application had been turned down by this pastor.

"No," Rev. Martin responded, "You think you know what you believe, but your beliefs are those of your parents. You wear them as a cloak. You've never been allowed to think for yourself. You've not internalized what you believe and don't believe. If you ever encounter a difficult situation, your beliefs will not stand the test. They're too superficial." Malcolm was angry. Only later, after living on his own, did Malcolm realize the truth of what Rev. Martin told him.

Internalization of faith occurs when we're allowed to think for ourselves. Throughout childhood, and especially in adolescence, we embark on a passionate pilgrimage to define a separate and whole "I." Questioning and exploring alternative ways of perceiving life become a part of the pilgrimage. For the most part, the strong beliefs taught to us will be adopted, but some may be discarded as we learn to think for ourselves.

Especially during the adolescent years, young people need to be encouraged to think for themselves and form their own opinions, even if they don't agree with adults in charge. More and more, they need the freedom to experience the consequences of the decisions that they make. Sometimes this may appear to be rebellion toward the parents or the teacher, but there's a difference between healthy rebellion—when a child begins to think for himself—and unhealthy rebellion. Disagreements may arise, but the wise parent or teacher knows how to ride the waves of disagreement rather than react punitively as the young person struggles to find answers. Listening, calm discussion, and unconditional love guide the rebellion into mature thinking.

As a young adult, Malcolm still faced the adolescent task of forming a solid sense of self, including those beliefs for which he would live—or yes, even die. Growing up under the sheltered roof of an authoritarian, punitive father and homeschooled by a strongly opinionated mother, the fear of consequences which had guided him as a child was no longer sufficient. Heeding the voices of what he'd been taught or following the natural inclinations of his own heart became a persistent dilemma in his search for what he believed. Going away to college, finding a job, and taking advantage of opportunities to meet those who's beliefs and lifestyles differed from his own sheltered existence furthered his quest for an authentic sense of self, but he made some serious mistakes along the way.

Now remorseful for those mistakes, Malcolm realized that what Rev. Martin had told him so long ago was true. Desperate to find a faith of his own, Malcolm began attending church more regularly and participating in a Bible study group which encouraged open discussion. Most importantly, he maintained a daily quiet time with God. That quiet time became essential to Malcolm's efforts to distinguish God's voice more clearly. The childhood cloak of obedience gave way to a heart filled with gratitude and a desire to please his Lord. Malcolm eventually found a new mission field and God has blessed him richly. He continues to teach and minister to students in the college where he's now employed with a strong, sustaining faith in God.

Spiritual Prep: *Ephesians 4:13–15; Philippians 1:6–10; Colossians 1:9–12; 1 Peter 2:2–5*

All I'm Created to be

How have your beliefs changed from those you were taught and adopted as a child? Describe those changes below:

Set Free

Describe ten beliefs about life and God which you hold dear enough to live or die for. Number them as you list them.

Prayer: Keep me growing, Lord. Keep me open to new experiences and new ways of looking at life as You guide me and help me to develop a mature, stable faith. Help me discern between error and Your truth.

Exercise 2

....

SMALL MATTERS OF FAITH

If you remain in me and my words remain in you, ask
whatever you wish, and it will be done for you.
John 15:7, NIV

Tracy, a bright, engaging student, was telling me why she refused an invitation from a young man on campus to go to a local bar. She described how, when the thought of this invitation came to mind during her morning devotional time, she felt a "no" from God. Tracy said that when she was younger, she never thought that God might care about the small details of her life. She'd never expected Him to make Himself known to her in anything except major decisions and events. She believed that He couldn't be bothered with the trite encounters of her boring routine, so she went about her way, floundering and ill equipped to meet the demands made upon her daily.

It was out of repeated failure, Tracy said, that she turned to God and began to depend on Him in all matters, not just major decisions. As she did so, He showed her that He would, indeed, make His presence known to her in the details and small decisions she faced daily. Tracy described how she began to expect exciting results from praying about even the routine things in her life. A whole new world opened up to her. When problem situations, no matter how insignificant or significant, engulfed her, she lifted her thought to God and immediately became aware of His presence, guiding her and restoring clarity to the situation and confidence to her walk.

What joy this new discovery brought to Tracy! What a beautiful, new relationship with Him! As she attempted to listen for and abide by the guidance He gave in these lesser moments, He seemed to move within her heart and reconcile her life more and more to Him. Gradually, in the conscious awareness of lifting up day-by-day events to Him, God took the rough, protective shell behind which Tracy often hid and gently released all that was creative and bright in her. In small ways and seemingly insignificant moments, He taught her to love in a whole new way. Tracy told me that if she had never learned this lesson of giving Him the small details of her life, she shuddered to think how she would have missed knowing the riches of His abiding presence in all areas of her life.

God cares about small things. He cares about the meeting you're going to have with the co-worker, the lunch date you have with a friend, even what you'll talk about at that lunch. He cares about the music you choose, the movie you and your friend see, and whether or not you buy that new outfit. We're never too old to learn to trust Him with these small things. Start trusting Him. Then watch! Through such daily trust, you'll see Him do much bigger things in your life.

Spiritual Prep: *Psalm 37:23–24; Proverbs 16:3,9; Isaiah 58:11; Luke 12:6–7*

All I'm Created to be

List some of the major decisions which God has led you to make in your life:

Set Free

Now, take a few moments to think through the past twenty-four hours, beginning with when you woke up yesterday. List all the details in that period of time, no matter how small, about which you think God cares and why.

Prayer: Father, help me to listen for Your still, calm voice as You guide me in all the events which make up my day. Let me know that nothing is too small to bring to You for Your care and guidance.

Exercise 3

....

INVESTING IN FAITH

When Jesus heard this, he said to him, "You still lack one thing. Sell everything you have and give to the poor, and you will have treasure in heaven. Then come, follow me."
Luke 18:22, NIV

"But I'm the one who's poor," Jason blurted out as he repeated the above Scripture verse from his morning reading. Surviving on a part-time income while attending a small. private Christian college left Jason feeling that he was really impoverished. "Why did God give me this to read?" he asked. Jason exclaimed that he certainly didn't have to worry about being too wealthy to enter the kingdom of God! Insufficient funds had lately been a fast companion in his life.

As our discussion of this Scripture passage continued, Jason began to realize that he was not poor by any stretch of the imagination. His needs were barely but adequately met; his medical bills were covered by his parents' insurance; there was always food on his table; and he was even able to give a small amount to his church. True, he had few luxuries, but he wasn't poor in the real sense of the word. Digging deeper into his thoughts, Jason expressed gratitude for his part-time employment, family, friends, bright sunshine days, and studies at the college. He recognized that he had a church family that loved him and friends who inspired and uplifted him. He laughingly mentioned that he and his housemates had two fat, furry cats that purred and bounced on their laps whenever they had the chance and a sheepdog who misdirected his herding instinct toward the cats. And, Jason added, he had a clear mind and God-given insights. Suddenly, Jason was smiling at the abundance of riches in his life.

There are no possessions, no human relationships, no positions, no honors that we can obtain which will ever earn us one second of time in God's presence. There is nothing earthly that will create a more Christ-like nature within us. There's nothing that will ever exceed the joy of knowing Him, nor hold more purpose than serving Him.

It is a joyful day when our thoughts are no longer dominated by concern for earthly treasures—when our hearts seek first and always His kingdom and His righteousness. It's difficult for the rich man to enter the kingdom of God—the man who is rich in friends, in family, in prestige, in position, in being a part of a culture that offers so many material pleasures—because his mind is more often preoccupied with those things than with the God Who gave those blessings to him. Only by placing our faith and hope in our Lord Jesus Christ will we ever know the riches of being a part of His kingdom.

Spiritual Prep: *Proverbs 10:2, 22; Malachi 3:10; Matthew 6:19–21; 19:20–21; Luke 12:15; 2 Corinthians 9:8*

All I'm Created to be

Which of your possessions are most important to you?

Take a few minutes and talk with God about those things that are important to you. Ask Him if they are possessions He wants you to have in your life. Describe how you think God responds to your possessions.

Set Free

Make a list of many blessings as you can which God has given you:

Prayer: Lord Jesus, You have blessed my life so abundantly! But the greatest blessing of all is Your companionship. Thank You for making me rich in what really counts.

Exercise 4

....

GOD'S WILL VERSUS SELF-WILL

A brother wronged is more unyielding than a fortified city;
disputes are like the barred gates of a citadel.
Proverbs 18:19, NIV

The students involved in our campus ministry program decided to have an all-day evangelism emphasis on campus. Their goals were high, their dreams glorious, and their enthusiasm unlimited. They'd invited some eminent personalities to be part of the day's program and, although they'd not yet raised the necessary funds, the personalities had accepted.

Brandon, the campus minister, hoped the enthusiasm elicited by this event would result in spinoff ministries of regular campus prayer groups, discipleship training, and year-long evangelism. He became caught up in the plans of the students and the high hopes they had of "reaching the campus for Christ." He was totally unaware that trouble was about to begin.

In the midst of the clamor and busy preparation for this day, he answered his telephone one morning and found himself listening to a stern admonition from the minister of one of the larger churches in town. The financial contribution of the minister's church was vital for Brandon's entire campus ministry program, as well as for the special day's events the students were planning. The minister of this church objected strongly to the stance of one of the personalities invited. In fact, he threatened removal of his support of the entire campus ministry if this person was not removed from the program.

Angered by the minister's authoritarian tone, Brandon refused to give in to his demands. Harsh words were exchanged between the two ministers. Neither was willing to sit and discuss the issue and consider the views of the other. The disagreement reached other pastors who tried to negotiate with both the minister and with Brandon, but their respective egos prevailed. Much later, Brandon admitted that it was more hot-headed rebellion than faith which spurred him to encourage the students to continue with the personalities they'd scheduled for the program. Brandon eventually grew hostile and petty in his attitude toward this pastor, and no mutual agreement was ever reached.

God blessed the efforts of the students, but Brandon never tasted peace over that situation. Regardless of whether or not he'd been right, Brandon had lost a friend and a supporter for the campus ministry program. Brandon also lost his earlier enthusiasm for campus ministry and eventually for his own faith. He resigned his position and entered another college to study in an altogether different field. It was a year later before Brandon began to understand he'd allowed his own ego to destroy his ministry and almost destroy his faith. Eventually, Brandon allowed the light of God's truth to reach him; he realized he'd acted on his own strong will and not on God's guidance. Brandon confessed to God the stubbornness of his actions and, in doing so, finally found peace and purpose in his life once again.

When we let self-will and stubbornness drive us toward achieving our own ends, then it's our ego with which we're concerned and not God's will. Regardless of how justified we might feel in our opinion, God sees the bigger picture and knows what's best for all concerned. Taking the situation in our own hands and demanding that God justifies our words and actions is actually a rejection of faith in Him. Trusting Him to meet our needs, as well as the needs of those involved, may mean relinquishing our plans and allowing Him to lead us along an unexpected path. Faith is the willingness to travel that path, even when it doesn't seem to meet our desires nor be to our advantage.

Spiritual Prep: *1 Samuel 15:23; Psalm 78:7–8; James 3:13-18*

All I'm Created to be

What has been your greatest accomplishment? Describe the role God played in it:

Set Free

What do you believe you can do, with God's guidance, to make the world a little better?

Prayer: Lord Jesus, help me to recognize the difference between stubbornness and faith, between my ego and Your gentle voice. Give me the wisdom and strength to relinquish plans that are not part of Your will and seek Your path for my life.

Exercise 5

....

A LIFETIME QUEST

Have I not commanded you? Be strong and courageous. Do not be afraid; do not
be discouraged, for the LORD your God will be with you wherever you go.
Joshua 1:9, NIV

Elizabeth told me that many times, good and bad, while growing up, she thought that she'd arrived at all of life's answers: when she accepted Christ at age eleven; when a high school friend deceived her; when she took a religion class in her freshman year of college; when she lost her job, and on and on. With each new situation, whether she successfully encountered it or failed miserably, she kept thinking each new insight gained was the last and there was no more to be learned!

"Ah," Elizabeth thought, "now I understand who I am and what this life is all about. I've finally reached my goal and will be able to handle anything life throws at me. It'll be clear skies from now on: no more mistakes, no more misunderstanding on my part. I know what to do now!" And then, she told me, she would run smack into a wall. She would find herself in another troubled relationship or find herself in an unsolvable situation or she'd catch herself seriously doubting God. Mind bruised and head spinning, Elizabeth would wonder how this could've happened. She would be, she added, once again unsure of herself, less certain of the future, and questioning her faith.

We don't suddenly have all the answers when we become Christians. Mistakes, misunderstandings, and misperceptions continue throughout any lifetime. God promises to be with us in all circumstances. He offers us the clear mindedness, strength, and compassion to cope—but not necessarily immediate answers. I've frequently been aware of His presence strengthening me and giving me insight into troubled events, and sometimes I've been aware of His intervention in those circumstances. Because of my experiences, however, my faith does not rest well on the expectation that He will make all answers immediately clear or banish all of my problems.

Life remains a struggle for most Christians. It involves the daily effort to understand, to walk wisely, to grow in His will, to love others, to serve Him. I suspect that it's okay, even wise, to recognize that life is often fearful and that our own individual pilgrimage means confronting this fear. When we confront the misunderstandings, failures, hurts, anger, boredom—and yes, joys—we grow. When we acknowledge that no magical power will dissipate all problems nor elevate us beyond their touch, we can learn from them.

We can choose to open our hearts and minds to His guidance in the experiences which make up our reality. We can let the pain or joy of the moment be a winnowing tool, or we can turn from Him because the answers aren't clear. I believe—and have tasted of this myself—that if we consciously choose to rely on God when we face problems, He is with us in His power, in His strength, and in the fullness of His love. He doesn't necessarily provide all the answers on our schedule—and sometimes His answer is "no"—but He will always help us to understand and grow from the problems that we experience. As He manifests His presence to us, somehow we take a step closer to Him in our pilgrimage. In this there is victory and, in this, there is joy.

Spiritual Prep: *2 Chronicles 15:4; Psalms 9:9; 27:5; 138:7–8, Luke 12:7; James 1:5-6*

All I'm Created to be

List some ages and periods in your life when you thought you had found all the answers to life:

List some questions with which you currently struggle:

Set Free

Spend time in prayer, lifting each of the above questions up to God. Expect God to answer. It may be immediately, tomorrow, or ten years from now when He answers, but He will answer! When He does, use this book to record His answer to your questions.

Prayer: Lord Jesus, when I face problems and have questions, remind me that, although You may not give me an immediate answer nor alter the circumstances, You are with me in those circumstances and will help me to find answers.

STEP SEVEN

Living The Christian Life: Prayer

Exercise 1

....

PRAYER PROMISES

For no matter how many promises God has made, they are "Yes" in Christ.
And so through him the "Amen" is spoken by us to the glory of God.
2 Corinthians 1:20, NIV

I bent down to soothe the small puppy beside the door of the mission church as I arrived to teach Sunday school. It was a freezing winter morning. Ice covered everything, and the little brown pup with huge black eyes stood outside the mission door, shivering so hard that he would topple over and have to jump upright again. He begged to go inside to the warmth, so the children and I took him into the trailer and wrapped him in a dry towel for a little while before putting him back outside. But he seemed to have nowhere to go and quickly become covered with the sleeting ice again.

I surveyed the homes in the little village. He belonged to no one. Nor could I impose on the people of this impoverished mountain community to take him into their homes. There was certainly no food to be spared for an animal. The puppy whimpered so mournfully when I once again reached down to brush his fur clean of the ice that I was unable to leave him stranded outside the mission without food or warmth. I took him home with me.

What a bright little animal he was! I named him Laddie. But I was still without a place to keep him. The faculty housing in which I lived wouldn't accept animals and I certainly couldn't move in the dead of winter. Knowing that it was almost impossible to find a home for a stray animal in this town, I decided to ask God for help with the small puppy. "Father," I prayed, "I know this is a very small matter and that there are much more urgent needs in this world, but would You help me find a home for Laddie?"

Within the week, I received a call from a new minister in town. His children had just lost their beloved companion, a collie which had been with the family since the children's birth. He heard about the puppy from a student whom I taught and was wondering if he could adopt it. Months later, I had the joy of seeing Laddie again. He was almost fully grown, sprawled on the front porch of his new family's home, and encircled by the arms of two very loving children.

The story of Laddie is recorded in the "answered prayer" section of my journal. At the time I wrote it, I was positive that God had taken that situation in His hands. But, typical for me, I didn't sustain the certainty for long. Faced with other problems and needs in my life, I once again began to doubt that He had heard or would answer my prayers.

It has taken me many years to learn to rely, still sometimes reluctantly, on His promises. But as I've come to do so, a change has taken place in my life and work. There's a peace of mind and quiet confidence now regardless of external circumstances. In Him, we truly have an anchor for our lives. It's enough that Christ bore our sins on the cross and that before him we stand totally clean and pure, forgiven, loved, accepted. But there is more. He will meet all our needs and fill the empty places of our hearts. He will respond to our prayers. He will keep His promises.

Spiritual Prep: *1 Kings 8:56; Romans 4:20–21; 2 Corinthians 7:1; Hebrews 10:23; 2 Peter 3:9*

All I'm Created to be

Describe a time when God specifically answered a prayer promise He made to you:

Set Free

Describe some prayers you're still waiting for God to answer. (When He answers, be sure to record it!)

Prayer: Lord, accept my gratitude. Thank you for seeing my needs and meeting them in ways You know best. You are the anchor of my soul. You are the peace in my life. You are the joy in my heart. Thank You for being a prayer-answering God.

Exercise 2

....

RECOGNIZING AND AVOIDING MANIPULATION

And when you pray, do not keep on babbling like pagans, for they
think they will be heard because of their many words.
Matthew 6:7, NIV

God doesn't apply Band-Aids®. His is a deep healing process. Many times, in our shortsighted perception of life, we want quick cures and bandages. We pray and pray, and wonder why God doesn't answer our prayers. Perhaps, we think, we've just not made ourselves clear enough about how much we need this thing. Perhaps we just haven't come up with the exact, right words. Somehow, we feel, we must make God aware of the validity and urgency of our request. Then, surely, He'll give us the answer we want.

The purpose of prayer is not to coerce or persuade God, not to inform God, nor to manipulate, force, or obligate God. The purpose of prayer is to know God and His will, to surrender to Him. We can't bargain with God, nor is there any magic in saying the right words or repeating a prayer a particular number of times. Even constancy in prayer, while an admirable trait, is not the key to getting our prayers answered. In prayer, we open our hearts to God as we would to a trusted friend, talk to Him, but also listen to Him. Listening, waiting on the Lord silently with open hearts and minds, gives us greater insight into His will. We find Him moving powerfully in our lives, increasing our confidence in His love for us, and giving us assurance when we listen to Him.

The parable of the friend who was approached at midnight (Luke 11:5–9) is not told to encourage redundancy in prayer. It's more a parable of contrasts rather than comparison. Instead of making a correlation between the reluctant friend and Christ, it's better for us to view Christ's mercy and receptiveness in contrast to the sleepy resistance of the friend. Unlike the friend, Christ is always ready to hear us, always ready to respond to our petitions. Conversations with the Father are encouraged at all times—not nagging. We can't, as a child might do with a parent, cajole and coax Him to do what we want.

How wonderful to bring our needs and leave them at the feet of Christ. In this we find peace. He hears our heart's longing. He knows us and cares for us. When all else is stripped from us so that our wounds are left bare and cold, and all we have is our faith in God, the awesome certainty that he will answer floods our heart and submerges us in the joy of His presence.

Spiritual Prep: *1 Chronicles 16:11; Psalm 145:18; Matthew 6:7–8; Romans 8:26;*
Ephesians 6:17,18; Colossians 4:2

All I'm Created to be

Imagine a God who is perfectly just, but never merciful. Describe how that God would answer prayers:

Now, think about a God who is merciful and loving but does not care about justice. Describe how that God would answer prayers:

Finally, think about our God who is both perfectly merciful and perfectly just. Describe the differences that would make in how God answers prayer:

Set Free

List five personal needs in order of importance. Think about how a God who is both loving and just would respond to those needs. List the needs and how you think He would respond below:

Prayer: Father, help me to rest in the assurance that You hear all of my prayers, and that you will answer each of them according to Your will. Teach me to not try to manipulate you into doing what I want. Instead, help me to accept Your direction for my life and to walk in obedience to Your will.

Exercise 3

....

THE HOLY SPIRIT AND PRAYER

But when he, the Spirit of truth, comes, he will guide you into all the truth. He will not speak
on his own; he will speak only what he hears, and he will tell you what is yet to come.
John 16:13, NIV

Ginger had just experienced a small taste of victory and wanted to share it with me. After persistent nudging by the Holy Spirit, she consciously obeyed God's gentle guidance yesterday— and felt great about it!

She'd spent hours writing and revising a summary report of her campus ministry activities for the previous month and was ready and eager to send it to her employers. She confessed to me that she's pretty hard-headed and didn't exactly have the purest of motivations in writing the report. She wanted those who employed her to be impressed and, well, even a little awed by all the progress she'd made. Besides, she was upset with a few of those who had received previous reports. She felt they hadn't demonstrated appropriate enthusiasm for what she'd done and for the projects she'd undertaken.

Ginger didn't send the narrative. She wanted to. But the Spirit kept whispering, "No." Even though reasoning urged her to mail it, she backed off from acting on "common sense" and acted, instead, on the still, small, but persistent voice of God. God frequently uses common sense and good judgment to guide us. Our minds and our intelligence are both gifts from God. We need to develop these gifts as surely as we would develop any gift He bestows. And what a joy it is when God's Spirit affirms our reasoning! What certainty that gives us in our decisions! However, there are times that the Spirit may counteract even our good, common sense. It takes quietness, strength, humility, and a listening ear ever tuned to God to hear the heartfelt voice of His Spirit. After more than forty years, Ginger admitted she was only beginning to learn to discern it.

In addition to her own natural stubbornness, Ginger was not exposed to those who spoke much of the Holy Spirit until her adult years. She told me that it was almost as if He were a family member about whom she wasn't allowed to talk. He was there, but He wasn't allowed to come out into the open too often. Ginger was led to believe that people might get the wrong impression of the family if she talked about the joy of the Spirit too frequently or too eagerly acknowledged His role in her prayer life. Heaven forbid if she ever raised her hands in worship, sang too exuberantly, or clapped in the sheer joy of His presence. People might get the wrong idea! It was almost presented as a choice she was forced to make: between being an intelligent, thinking, stable person, or a person who expressed the joy of being filled with the Holy Spirit. I agreed with Ginger that churches which stifle the movement of the Spirit are missing a great deal! What a delight it is to find an intelligent individual who opens her life to the Holy Spirit without fear of people's reactions to the manifestation of God's Spirit in her thoughts, words, and actions.

Many times, Ginger admits she still goes her own way, ignoring the gentle nudging of the

Holy Spirit, until disaster sets in. But when she does listen . . . oh, the joy, the triumph, the rightness of it. His Spirit is with us to guide us into all truth if we take the time to listen.

Spiritual Prep: *Romans 8:26; Ephesians 5:18; 6:18; Colossians 3:16; Jude 1:20*

All I'm Created to be

Describe a time when the Holy Spirit nudged you to take a specific path. What was the outcome? What did the Spirit teach you, as a result?

Set Free

Think quietly for a few moments about the areas of your life where you depend upon the guidance of the Holy Spirit. Describe them below.

Where do you sense the Spirit calling you to depend more upon Him now? What do you think that would look like? Write your thoughts below.

Prayer: Father, what joy the presence of Your Holy Spirit brings to my life! Help me to listen, to be sensitive to His guidance, and to rejoice in whatever direction He leads.

Exercise 4

....

SURPRISED BY PRAYER

As the deer pants for streams of water, so my soul pants for you,
my God. My soul thirsts for God, for the living God.
Psalm 42:1–2a, NIV

Once I read a short novel about a young widow who chose to join a charity group. This woman later became a martyr for her faith. Touched and inspired by the story, I wanted to give my heart to God in the same pure and total way demonstrated by that young woman. How I wished for the Christian qualities of that widow. My motive was sincere. The glory of being a martyr wasn't my desire, but the longing for her dedication and singular love of God was overwhelming.

In moments of disclosure, God sometimes speaks so directly that the impact of His presence leaves us stunned. Such an incident—small, but revealing—happened soon after this. My desire to live as this young woman had not been an urgent prayer request, although it'd been a sincere one. Perhaps it was the insignificant nature of these circumstances that sharpened the clarity of His response to me.

Despite the brevity of the book, the impression made by the story stayed with me. Two days after finishing the book, with the longing still fresh and undiminished in my heart, I began my regular morning devotions. The reading that morning was about the same young widow portrayed in the book. This was no coincidence! Instantly, I knew: God had heard my heart's desire. The impact and clarity of His response was intense. I was almost blinded for a moment to the rest of the reading while I sat, as it were, face to face with God. My heart literally sang His praises in those few moments. It really didn't matter what the rest of the reading said. I knew God cared. I knew He was with me and was listening to my every thought. Without a doubt, I knew He was letting me know that He had heard my heart's desire and that He approved.

How beautiful to realize that God walks this close to us, that He will communicate so clearly. As you spend time alone with God, perhaps you will realize that:

- Prayer helps you make choices.
- Prayer motivates you.
- Prayer gives you a solid place to unload your burdens.
- Prayer increases your faith and gives you confidence.
- Prayer improves your relationships.
- Prayer is a continual journey, through which you deepen your relationship with God.
- You, too, will be surprised by prayer and by an encounter with Him.

Through prayer, I've come to realize that any sincere desire to be more like Him, to become more the people He created us to be—will be heard and answered. But oh, the joy of knowing that He will speak with such directness! He will hear our cry to be His servants, to love him, and to obey Him; and He will point the way, strengthen us, and commune with us as we travel with Him, side by side.

Spiritual Prep: *Psalm 33:9; Isaiah 58:9a; Luke 12:12; 1 Corinthians 2:10–11*

All I'm Created to be

Describe some effects that prayer has had in your life in the past:

Set Free

In Revelation 3:20 Jesus said, "Behold, I stand at the door and knock." Pretend that you are home for the day and Jesus is visiting the neighborhood. He has just knocked on your living-room door. Close your eyes for several minutes and visualize this. Then answer the following questions:

1. What will you say to Him when he appears at your door?

2. Will you let Him in? Why or why not?

3. What is He going to ask you?

4. What questions are you going to ask Him?

5. Is there a room in your home that you do not want him to see? Why?

6. Are there any closets, drawers, photos, or computer files that you want to hide from Him? Again, why?

Stop again, close your eyes and allow Him to visit with you for five minutes. Visualize the visit. When five minutes are up, describe the visit below:

Prayer: Jesus, how wonderful is Your companionship. How marvelous it is when I can hear Your voice so clearly! Thank You for reminding me that You're personally involved in my life.

Exercise 5

....

POWER OF PRAYER

He gives strength to the weary and increases the power of the weak.
Isaiah 40:29, NIV

The television news focused on a fireman as he threw a rope to a young teenage boy. The adolescent secured the rope on something in the dark, smoke-filled room and clambered down to safety. As I watched this remarkable rescue, I thought, "How like that rope prayer can be." Prayer is the lifeline provided by God for each of us. When we're weary and feel like we're facing impossible odds, when the fires of our lives threaten to overwhelm us—that's when we most need to stop and reach out to Him through prayer. He is waiting to rescue us from weaknesses we cannot conquer and problems we cannot solve.

Sometimes the weight of the world—the pressures, the deadlines, and the expectations placed on us—so crowd us that it's difficult to make the time to spend alone with God, and because of that our hands slip from the very lifeline we need. We reach a point where we feel so tired, exhausted, and discouraged that life becomes an unwanted burden rather than an exciting pilgrimage spent growing in Christ. We use up all our energy and spend all our time fighting the fires of the world, leaving us discouraged and disinclined to spend time with Him. We give up the very lifeline we need most.

Too often, it's only after I've become exhausted with my own efforts that I finally turned to look into God's face to ask Him what's happening—only to find Him waiting to throw me a lifeline. At these moments, I've realized that it was because I had depended so much on my own pathetic strength that I exhausted myself. Without going to Him in prayer, seeking His will, I had rushed to put out the blaze of fire and found my eyes filled with smoke and my lungs gasping for a clean breath of air. But if we make an effort to lift our eyes to Him—no matter how dire our circumstances—we'll find that he holds out this rope of life for us.

Prayer is our connection with God—our strength, our lifeline to heaven! Prayer affects every aspect of a person: mind, body, and spirit. Research in the medical field has shown the power of prayer in the healing process and recovery of patients. Prayer is potent. No matter what's happening to us —whether we're experiencing the fires of disease, pain, loss, failure—we have a rope on which to grab: prayer.

God does seem, so often, to choose the weak and helpless through whom to do His mighty works. Perhaps it's because in these individuals there can be no vaunting of human effort—only a simple, upward cry of need toward which He can cast His lifeline of love.

Spiritual Prep: *Psalms 34:17; 50:15; 55:16–18; 86:5–7; 9*

All I'm Created to be

Describe a time when you witnessed the power of prayer in your or someone else's life.

Set Free

In what situations do you need God to throw you a lifeline now? What might that look like?

Prayer: My energy is exhausted, and I am so tired from doing things in my own strength. Remind me, Father, that You are waiting to throw a lifeline to me. Teach me to grab hold through prayer.

STEP EIGHT

Living The Christian Life: Witnessing

Exercise 1

....

MOTIVATION

"You are my witnesses," declares the LORD, "and my servant whom I have chosen,
so that you may know and believe me and understand that I am he."
Isaiah 43:10, NIV

There's not anyone whom God choses to leave out of His redemptive plan for mankind. Every person is a special creation of God, and He longs after each person as any parent would long after his child. As Christians, we're a unique source of introduction to this heavenly Father and to His Son who died on the cross for our sins. But what does it mean to be a witness? And how do we go about this task of witnessing?

You don't need training to become a witness. You've probably been witnessing for years, perhaps without even realizing it, by the type of life you lead. You may not be aware of all the people who've been watching and learning from you, but you're already a witness to something. The question is: To what have you been witnessing? What do people see when they're watching you? Do they see somebody who has seen and heard and felt the power of Jesus Christ? Living a life that reflects our Lord can lead others to change and to accept the gift of grace that He offers.

When you know Jesus Christ—when you've heard Him and when He has touched your life—you can tell about Him. That is far more important than knowing doctrines or formulas. A witness tells about what he or she has personally seen and heard. Your story—your testimony about what you have seen and felt God do in your own life—is the most powerful tool at your disposal for sharing the gospel

You may not have all the methods and books and angles in your grasp; you may not even know the doctrines of the church you attend. But if you've been walking with Jesus Christ, you've got something to say. What's more, you're never alone in this. The Holy Spirit has been sent into the world to bear witness to Christ, and the Holy Spirit is in you. You can be a firsthand living testimony to Jesus Christ through the power of the Holy Spirit.

Sadly, we've all encountered a few misguided Christians who felt that witnessing meant that they must convert others to their particular set of doctrines, believing that new converts could not possibly belong to the family of God otherwise. These witnesses seemed more concerned with chalking up the numbers and convincing others of their own perception of the Christian experience rather than sharing Christ's love. If you've encountered this type of witness, it almost feels as if they've a need to impose their own yokes onto the shoulders of new converts. I suspect that this need to convince others of the validity of their doctrines and burdens reflects their own self-doubts about the rituals they try so hard to follow.

Once you've shared the love that Christ demonstrated on the cross, leave it up to the Holy Spirit to do the convincing. Jesus didn't call us to impose our personal yokes and doctrines on others, but to introduce others to Him. He called us to the joy and freedom of sharing His love with others. As we draw nearer to God, our yokes assume less importance. Instead, we desire that God becomes everything to every person. The peace that we experience in our walk with Christ is the peace we want for everyone. We wish to share the joy and confidence that accompanies His presence abiding with us. His compassion and concern for all mankind becomes our concern. Out of that concern, we desire to tell others the wonderful news of Christ's death on the cross for the forgiveness of our sins.

Spiritual Prep: *Psalms 119:171–172; 145:2–7; Isaiah 44:8; Matthew 5:16*

All I'm Created to be

In the following space, write your testimony of how you came to accept Christ and what this has meant for your life. Include the time, place, circumstances, and persons involved. Use extra paper as needed.

Set Free

Rehearse your testimony aloud a few times. Then, ask some Christian friends to listen as you share your testimony with them. Continue practicing until you feel completely comfortable sharing your testimony. Ask God to provide opportunities for you to share your testimony with others—and begin looking out for these opportunities, trusting that God will be with you.

Prayer: God, keep me ever mindful of the difference between man's traditions and Your truth. Make my concern to be to share Your love with others, not to make them live the Christian life as I live or view it.

Exercise 2

....

PREPARATION

Now that you have purified yourselves by obeying the truth so that you have
sincere love for each other, love one another deeply, from the heart.
1 Peter 1:22, NIV

My grandmother (on my father's side) lived in an old two-story, rough-hewed plank home in the backwoods of North Carolina. Nothing extravagant, but it was a nice house adequate for the seven children raised in it. A large wooden porch surrounded the house. Next to the back door always sat a large, sparkling clean, tin bucket. I can remember many hot summer afternoons spent playing in the yard behind that house. Sweaty and tired after a day of "hide-n'-seek" or "cowboys-n'-Indians," we would rush to the bucket, and with the shiny silver dipper hanging beside it, scoop out some of the freshest, sweetest, coolest water you've ever tasted. Grandmother always made certain that the bucket was filled to the brim with water so we could enjoy its cool refreshment.

In the same way, I've found that I need to be "filled" with God's love before I can share it with others. Every day with a cup of hot tea, and with my Bible and journal in hand, I sit facing the window as the sun's first warming rays creep like soft fingers into the dark coolness of the early morning sky. I enjoy spending the first hour of each day with God when my thoughts are clearest and my needs most apparent. My mind is more receptive to whatever material I read during that first, fresh hour of each new day, and retains it longer. I want the content of that material to be conversations between God and I.

It's during these precious morning times that I ask God to warm my heart with His presence and cleanse me from sin. It's during this time, before I become lost in the business of the day, that I read His Word. I'm most aware of and comforted by His Holy Spirit in the morning, without whom my witness would be meaningless. Only by the work of His Spirit through me will others be drawn to Him. Only by the work of the Holy Spirit will words and programs, inspired by Him, take hold and meet the needs of a hurting world.

As I allow myself to be guided by God's Spirit throughout my day, I often find myself reminding students that, even though I am willing to work with them, their best teacher and counselor is God. Certainly no one knows the mind of each person better than Him. God is the source of all life; He is the great healer. When I counsel, I recognize that I must allow His love and His truth to reach through my stumbling efforts to heal this troubled person.

The tools of my trade are of little value apart from Him. While He may use my hands and my words, it is still God, through Christ, who soothes the troubled heart and brings hope out of wilted dreams. He will reach into past hurts to bind old wounds and forgive errant ways. I can only serve as the facilitator who helps others to rise above their life circumstances and come to rest at the feet of Christ. Having spent the morning hours in His presence, I'm more able to direct others to their true Source of help.

Spiritual Prep: *Joshua 1:8–9; Lamentations 3:22–23; Acts 1:8*

All I'm Created to be

Write out a schedule for your complete day below. Include a time for devotions in your schedule. Please allow the remainder of this page as space after this question

Set Free

List the materials that you currently use and/or will need for your devotional times (i.e., notebook, pen, Bible, devotional magazines, books, etc.). Then gather those items in a spot that is quiet and private, where you will meet God each day at the time specified in your schedule.

Prayer: Lord Jesus, help me to set aside time each day to spend with You and to remain faithful to keeping that time. During these quiet moments, fill my heart to the brim with Your love so that I can't help but let it spill over to others.

Exercise 3

....

THE OFFENSIVE WITNESS

When pride comes, then comes disgrace; but with humility comes wisdom.
Proverbs 11:2, NIV

Early in my college teaching career, I encountered Luke. Upon first meeting him, Luke was not unpleasant to be around, but he seemed to eventually alienate almost everyone with whom he came in contact. His approach to sharing the good news of Christ was in-your-face abrasive. He attacked and belittled the other person's beliefs. The gospel seemed like a weapon in his hands.

And perhaps he needed this weapon. Luke's mother had died shortly after his birth, and he'd been abandoned by his father. I found myself wishing that he would seek counseling and even attempted to gently suggest this to him. However, his pride left no room for admission of such a need. Nor did it leave time for him to admit the need to study in order to complete his college classes.

Slowly, but clearly, Luke was destroying his own opportunities to minister for Christ. His grades dropped. He not only got himself blocked from visitation rights at the local hospital and juvenile home, but his reputation caused the doors to be barred against other students from the college who wished to do visitation. His pride—a protection from his own feelings of insecurity and fear of failure—was disgracing him and bringing ill repute on other Christians associated with him.

I believe that Luke longed to be called a friend and a child of God. I remain hopeful that he will achieve this reputation in his lifetime. But at the time I knew him, his unresolved problems dominated his personality. Someday, perhaps, when he's willing to face those problems and come to grips with his fear and insecurity, when he faces his anger at those who abandoned him, God will take the hurt and the potential for growth and turn Luke into a truly mighty witness for Him.

How do people respond to your attempts to witness? If they reject your testimony, be careful not to become argumentative nor to despair. The same God who calls us also enables us. By simple faith in Christ—by putting our hands in His and giving our lives to Him—He will strengthen us, fill us with His Spirit, and guide us as we attempt to witness for Him. We can only share what we know and have experienced. We have to wait on the Holy Spirit to convince.

Although we're motivated by a deep desire to share God's love and grace, we must understand that only God can change hearts and minds. You may mourn the tragic loss of God's truth for the individual who refuses to accept it. But remember—that person, that program, is in God's hands. Leave the results with God.

Spiritual Prep: *1 Samuel 17:47; 2 Chronicles 20:15; Romans 16:17–18; 2 Corinthians 2:14–15; Galatians 5:22–23; 6:9; Hebrews 10:24*

All I'm Created to be

Describe a situation in which you tried to be a witness but was rejected:

How did this make you feel?

Set Free

Describe a situation in which you'd like to be able to witness:

Now, spend some time in prayer, lifting up that situation and asking God to give you the opportunities and courage to be a witness. When you've finished praying, describe how you'd feel most comfortable witnessing in that situation:

Prayer: Father, help me to be a courageous witness, with respect, love, and compassion for the other person's feelings. Remind me often that, although I may be the one who is witnessing, it is the Holy Spirit who draws others to You.

Exercise 4

....

FINDING THE RIGHT WORDS

He then said to me: "Son of man, go now to the people of Israel and speak my words to them."
Ezekiel 3:4, NIV

Beth and Sandra had been friends for more than a year. When Beth became a Christian, she was eager to tell Sandra about her new faith. The next day when they met over coffee, Beth was surprised to learn that Sandra had been a Christian for many years. When Beth asked Sandra why she never spoke of it, Sandra replied that she wasn't sure what to say. Beth thought of all the heartache she'd encountered in the previous year and wondered how much of it might have been avoided if only Sandra had told her about Christ.

If it were left up to our abilities, or if we had to become holy enough to witness, then there would be an authentic reason to remain silent. However, the same God who calls us also enables us. By simple faith in Christ—by putting our hands in His and giving our lives to Him—He will strengthen us, fill us with His Spirit, and give us the words as we attempt to witness for Him.

When we hear about something really new and exciting, catch it on TV, or read about it on Facebook, we can't wait to share it. We're eager to tell our friends and close acquaintances and, if the news is good enough, we even want strangers to benefit from it. It's that same excitement, that same concern for others that drives us to witness. God's forgiving, redemptive love offered to us through Christ's death on the cross is the best news anyone will ever hear. Our world is a hurting place and, wherever we are, people are desperate for forgiveness and healing in their lives. As Christians, we hold in our hands the secret of that forgiveness and healing. We've experienced the joy of being adopted into God's family, and the peace and happiness which He provides is sufficient and full and will spill over to those around us—if we let it.

Your circumstances provide you with your mission field. There are so many who've heard only a partial or distorted version of the truth. While it's probably accurate to say that the most observable and consistent witness you can offer is your behavior and lifestyle, there are times when you'll need to openly speak about Christ's role in your life. A natural and comfortable acknowledgment of God's love, through the guidance of His Holy Spirit, is all that's needed. While some may make good use of packaged materials or formats for sharing God's grace, you can simply rely on the Holy Spirit to show you the way that's best for you.

The mature Christian lifestyle is so filled with His Spirit that we long to share His joy with those with whom we live, work, and play. How fulfilling to be so intimately involved with our Heavenly Father that we've no fear of speaking His name nor revealing our relationship with Him. How marvelous and exciting to know that He is using our actions and our words to attract others to the Christ whose Spirit dwells within us.

Spiritual Prep: *Exodus 4:11–12; Psalm 35:28; Ecclesiastes 3:7; Luke 12:12; Acts 18:9–10*

All I'm Created to be

List ten people with whom you'd like to share the good news of Jesus:

Set Free

In the space above, next to their names, write what you'd like to say to each of the ten people you just listed.

Prayer: Lord Jesus, nudge my heart when a verbal witness is appropriate. Put the words in my mouth that will draw others close to you.

STEP NINE

Living The Christian Life: Purpose

Exercise 1

....

INTERPRETING OUR CALL

Now to him who is able to do immeasurably more than all we ask or imagine . . .
Ephesians 3:20, NIV

"Pat, this is Pastor Jim. I was wondering if you'd play the piano for our nursing home ministry. We're pretty desperate for someone to play."

"You must be desperate if you want to subject them to my piano playing," I laughed.

Among any talents I have, music is the least developed. But I enjoy playing the piano, even though my hearing impairment limits my ability to master the skill. So I began to play for the nursing home ministry. What dear hearts the residents were! Never once did they complain about my frequent wrong notes; they just loved to sing! And I found the weekly hour at the nursing home to be one of the highlights of my week.

"It's not your abilities that God wants but your availability," declares a popular poster. We're all called to be His ministers. Whether a student, housewife, professional, retired person, missionary, or church pastor, it's not the skills on which we pride ourselves that matter; it's our availability to Him.

Through our walk with Jesus Christ, we flower into people with all the beauty with which God imbued us. God made us, and He created that which is lovely in our being. Only He can bring to fruition all He means for us to be. The world certainly won't. The world will lead us on a path that inhibits, distorts, and destroys that which is good in us. But as we make our lives available to God, we may find ourselves caught by surprise at the talents He brings out in us and the opportunities He provides for us to use them.

What can you give Him? An arm around a child's shoulder? A strong voice for reading stories?

Skills to lead a Bible study? All of us can do something for Jesus. Leaning on Him, the Author of all truth and beauty, He will encourage our hearts and minds and show us how to use that which is best in each of us. As we make ourselves available to God, our talents will take shape. With His guidance, we can live and work and love so that He is glorified.

Spiritual Prep: *Psalm 32:8–9; Proverbs 3:5–6; Galatians 6:10, Ephesians 4:1–3; 1 Peter 1:15–16*

All I'm Created to be

Special talents the Lord has given me:

Talents that I wish I had:

Set Free

Describe three ways you'd like to serve God, and identify the talents you'd need to do so:

Prayer: Father God, help me to identify my talents and show me how to use my abilities to Your glory!

Exercise 2

....

USING OUR TALENTS

The LORD is my strength and my shield; my heart trusts in him, and he
helps me. My heart leaps for joy, and with my song I praise him.
Psalm 28:7, NIV

My friend Bruce has a great tenor voice. It's the best I've ever heard. Yet, every effort by Bruce to use his talent has run into impossible barriers. Bruce even cut a record, but it didn't sell. Still, my friend continues to train and to sing whenever the opportunity presents itself.

I can listen to Bruce sing and know that he's praising God with his whole heart; his voice seems to float on angels' wings. How God must stop and listen with a smile on His face and with eyes shining with love each time Bruce sings. God will use that talent. Neither I nor my friend knows how or when. But that doesn't matter; Bruce continues to sing.

Ronald Dunn, in his book <u>When Heaven Is Silent</u>, makes a very good point: when your efforts are blocked, or you face a particularly difficult barrier, instead of asking "Why?" ask "What now?" The "why" may never be answered, but the "what now" takes our eyes off the past and gives us a future, a hope. It expresses our faith that God has our best interests in mind.

Have your efforts to use your skills and talents been rebuffed or ignored? Have you begun to doubt that you have any special abilities, and given up on using the gifts you once thought were yours? Do you think about hiding the skills He's given you, because you see no earthly way they can be used? No matter how discouraged you might be, don't give up. Continue to develop these talents. Discipline yourself. Trust Him to take the product of your effort and to use it to His glory. Find your own individual race and run it for Him. Then, when you lay down to rest at night, you'll do so with the peace that comes from knowing you've done all you can to use your God-given abilities. The rest is in His hands!

You can wake in the morning with praise on your lips and a song to Him in your heart. Work on making your skills the best they can be; let your thoughts dwell on Him as you exercise your talents; allow yourself to experience the joy of knowing you're doing your best for Him. Have confidence that because you've obeyed, He will bless your efforts. In Him, you have a future and a hope.

Spiritual Prep: *Psalm 1:3; Romans 12:6–8; 1 Corinthians 12:4–6; 1 Timothy 4:14*

All I'm Created to be

My dream for this world is:

Set Free

How can you use your talents to help make this dream come true?

Prayer: Father, fill my heart with the peace of knowing that I've done my best to develop and exercise my gifts. Assure me that You will use my efforts, although I may not see how at this moment.

Exercise 3

....

CHOOSING WHERE TO SERVE

Also, seek the peace and prosperity of the city to which I have carried you into exile. Pray to the LORD for it, because if it prospers, you too will prosper.
Jeremiah 29:7, NIV

It was a particularly pleasant summer afternoon. The sun was bright and there was a cool breeze outside, so I left the door to my garden apartment opened as I worked. I'd spent the earlier hours of the day hanging wallpaper in the kitchen of my new faculty apartment and getting to know some of the neighbors who dropped by to chat and hang wallpaper along with me. Later, I was able to catch up on correspondence that had been weeks behind and then attend evening services at church.

I felt good about being in this place. Although I was now in the western part of the country, far away from my longtime home on the East Coast, it felt right being here. A cocoon-like warmth surrounded me. I knew that I was in God's will. I was optimistic about teaching. It was and still is my favorite work, but I no longer wore the rose-colored glasses of my youth's ambition. I realized that here, too, there would be difficult times. And so it has been in all of the places to which He's called me to serve—both the joy filled days and those filled with difficult times. I've known the warm fellowship of working alongside giants in the Christian faith while, at the same time, having to cooperate with those who plotted and schemed to hold on to positions which demanded skills different from their own. I've faced the contradiction of having a job well-done ignored or perceived as a threat rather than encouraged. I've seen the reputation of many colleagues muddled by jealousy, gossip, and half-truths. I've felt the frustration of having integrity interpreted as disloyalty and responsibility seen as a lack of cooperation. But by God's grace, the difficulties in these places of service became opportunities to exercise faith. And the kinder, gentler folks became my people, my family.

Have you been apportioned a rocky, stern place to scatter seed? As God's servant, do you sow on unyielding ground? Don't despair, and don't doubt your call. Finish the task He's given you. If God has you in this place, there'll be lessons for you to learn as well as service rendered, both of which will draw you into a closer walk with Him. Lean heavily on Him. Search for His strength and His wisdom. He'll show you the way over the boulders that cause you to stumble. He is with you in your place of service and He'll not forsake you. And when it comes time to leave, He'll gently nudge your heart and show you the door to service elsewhere, so that you'll have no doubt about His direction for you.

Spiritual Prep: *Isaiah 6:8; Jonah 3:1–3; Matthew 24:14; 28:19–20; 1 Corinthians 16:9*

All I'm Created to be

Describe a difficult circumstance in which you tried to serve God, or would have liked to serve Him. What was the outcome of your efforts?

Looking back now, why do you think God allow events to unfold in the way He did?

Set Free

Where and how would you like to serve God in the future? What obstacles do you anticipate as you try to move into this area of service?

Prayer: Father, when I am in a difficult place and things aren't going as I'd hoped, help me to continue to serve You and to draw the support I need from Your abiding presence. Show me how to feel at home wherever You send me.

Exercise 4

....

EFFECTIVE SERVICE

He called out to them, "Friends, haven't you any fish?" "No," they answered. He
said, "Throw your net on the right side of the boat and you will find some."
John 21:5–6, NIV

After Ed graduated from our college, he accepted a position as a campus student minister. He dreamed of programs which involved students in student-led Bible studies, missions, and community service; however, he had encountered resistance from students more frequently than eager participation in the programs.

A dull cloud of doubt began to settle about Ed as he questioned himself and God. God had brought him to this place and given him these sheep to take care of, hadn't He? Why then was he beginning to feel like such a miserable failure? Everything he tried seemed to go wrong. Ed began to believe that he didn't have what it "took" to become an effective campus minister. He could see no response on the part of the students to his teaching or attempts to foster a campus ministry program.

Ed was facing his first trip to make to the national conference for campus ministers with mixed feelings. He was in awe of some of the well-known ministers whom he'd meet at the national conference. Several of them were even legendary. Ed felt he had a lot to learn from the more experienced, successful campus ministers, but he was embarrassed by his lack of progress in building up his own campus program.

At the conference, Ed found the participants to be as knowledgeable and interesting as he'd imagined. Because he was a newcomer, however, he tended to stand back and observe. Many of those attending were relating fascinating stories about events that occurred in their ministries and the number of students involved. Ed was even more impressed by the stories he heard and wondered if he could ever accomplish as much as the others.

Ed was taken completely by surprise when one elderly minister, well known in the field, approached him and said, "I've been trying to find out where you were because I've heard so much about you and the fantastic work you're doing." Ed told me that the surprise must have registered on his face as he managed to sputter some meaningless garble of appreciation for the compliment. He struggled to look professional and worthy of the remark. Ed laughed as he related that his confidence, in those few, short seconds, expanded rather remarkably. How quickly, Ed said, his self-image changed and he visualized himself as outstanding, perhaps destined to be a better campus minister than most. His youth and lack of experience was forgotten. He must have been doing pretty miraculous things, he thought, for news of his work to have reached the ears of this well-known minister!

It was later that night, Ed said, when he returned to his hotel room, shut out the social clatter, and turned quietly to an evening devotion that reality set in. Certainly, he possessed skills and talents of a sort, but these were gifts from God and had become fruitful only with the touch of the Master's hand. As Ed leaned on God, trusting Him and following His guidance, God had used Ed's efforts and made his work shine with God's glory even without Ed's awareness.

Ed was deeply grateful that God had let him know that his work had been effective and that Ed was, indeed, serving God. In the quietness of the moment Ed recognized that God was his strong refuge, and the source of all that he accomplished. God was responsible for Ed's success, Ed's joy—and Ed's confidence.

The power of God who loves sin-stained persons—the power of God who brings the winter storms and the new spring rains—the power of God who died on the cross for us and then rose again from the dead—that same great power of God can take our efforts and, through them, accomplish miracles. He will do marvelous things through you as you serve Him.

Spiritual Prep: *Micah 6:8; Acts 20:18–24; Galatians 6:14; Philippians 4:13*

All I'm Created to be

Describe a time when you tried to serve God but thought you had failed:

Looking back at that time, describe how God might have used you in that situation despite what you thought—or what God has revealed to you since that time:

Describe some successes you have experienced, with God's help:

Set Free

What do you hope to accomplish for God with the rest of your life?

Prayer: Lord Jesus, thank You for letting me know that I am special to You, and that you have given me unique talents and skills. Keep me mindful that I exercise my talents best when I look to You and allow You to work through me.

STEP TEN

Living The Christian Life Victoriously

Exercise 1

······································

SETTING NEW PRIORITIES

Jesus replied: "'Love the Lord your God with all your heart and with all your
soul and with all your mind.' This is the first and greatest commandment.
And the second is like it: 'Love your neighbor as yourself.'"
Matthew 22:37–39, NIV

Getting our priorities in order is an important task but not an easy one. In the above Scripture passage, a picture is drawn of the priority that others should take in our lives. Getting that picture into focus is more difficult if we believe ourselves unlovely, worthless, and hopeless. It's troubling that many folks think that humility means "self devaluation." If we accept this definition, we might, in a misguided attempt to be humble, avoid looking at our talents and positive qualities and focus only on our negatives.

This passage clearly shows how God expects us to prioritize "self" in the scheme of things. There's no hierarchy between us and others. In fact there's a secret for loving others. If we can forgive and love ourselves, even as Christ has forgiven and loved us, then it becomes so much easier to really love others! So, go ahead, allow God to show you how to love yourself and see how much simpler it becomes for you to love your spouse, your parent, your friend, and your neighbor.

While there's no hierarchy between ourselves and others in the above Scripture verse, there is, however, one important distinction: Both our love for others, and our love for the unique self God created us to be, are to be subordinate to our love for God. No one, parent, child, husband, wife, friend, can share the position God occupies in our affections. While we are not to belittle ourselves in a misguided attempt to be humble, we are instructed to love God first and to place all our earthly affections in His hands.

However impossible though it may seem, or excruciatingly painful to think about, we must also be willing to release those we love to God before our hearts can be right with Him. Only by releasing them can we completely know the fullness of Christ living within us. Then, glory! The truth becomes clear! Christ loves us as well as any dear folk whom we cherish more than we dreamed. But for us to cling to others out of our own needs rather than releasing them to God would destroy them in its demanding, possessive grasp. If we make others the source of our happiness, our lives will leave us disillusioned and bitter when they fail to live up to expectations which no person can meet. Looking to them for life's answers leads to despair and grudge carrying when they fail to fulfill that impossible task.

Humility means to completely trust God with our loved ones, our circumstances, and all that concerns us; to put everything and everyone into His hands without demanding a return for our affection or revenge for wrongs done to us. It is when we give our affections and our circumstances completely to God that we realize the authentic, affirming, unfathomable meaning of love. In giving up, we gain. In releasing, we attain. Only then will we walk freely and love freely as new creatures in Christ.

Spiritual Prep: *Deuteronomy 6:4–5; Matthew 10:37–39; Mark 12:29–31; 1 John 5:2–3*

All I'm Created to be

My top three priorities are:

My next ten priorities are:

Set Free

Look over the lists of priorities you just made. Spend a few minutes in prayer asking God if there are any changes in your priorities you feel He's leading you to make. Rewrite your priorities according to those changes:

Prayer: Lord Jesus, help me to set my priorities, so that they reflect Your priorities. Help me to love myself and others as You love and, to love and trust You supremely.

Exercise 2

....

REJOICING

This is the day which the LORD has made; let us rejoice and be glad in it.
Psalm 118:24, RSV

Spring has returned. A neighbor has just brought me a handful of her garden's daffodils. The cats are begging to go outside to chase the returning robins, and windows have been stripped of their winter glass to admit the soft, warm breeze. At the college, the students restlessly daydream away class lectures, or loll in pairs and small groups on the campus lawn. This is indeed a glorious day which the Lord has made, and it's easy to rejoice and be glad in it.

But what about the days when there are no fresh, spring breezes or warm sunshine, when there are no bright yellow daffodils or romantic thoughts about which to daydream? Did the Lord design these days also? Where is the cause for rejoicing and for being glad in them? During the long periods when the skies have been overcast for weeks and each day passes without any vision of green grass or new romance, where do we look to find evidence of His presence and feel the gentle touch of His love?

Perhaps the necessity for these days is in teaching us that the place to find Him is not only in the natural world around us, even with its breathtaking beauty, but in our walk, day by day, and minute by minute in His presence. Even the dreariest of days can be warmed by the presence of God's Spirit and by the grasp of His hand as we walk through the circumstances that crowd our lives. He is always with us, in drab days as well as bright ones. We only need to recognize His presence to grasp hope and joy again. There's nothing that man or nature can do to rob us of this joy. No one can take the eternal springtime from our hearts when they are filled with His love.

Spiritual Prep: *Psalms 42:11; 126:5–6; Isaiah 55:12; Jeremiah 31:13*

Living Free

Congratulations! *If you've completed this workbook, you've worked hard, and come a long way in finding and expressing the person God wants you to be!*

Now, find a photograph of yourself as an adult. If there is room on the inside front cover of this workbook, place it beneath the photo of you as a child; if there isn't room, attach it to the inside of the back cover. As you go through the next twenty-four hours, allow God to remind you of your value to Him. Look for ways that God touches your heart and record them here before you go to bed:

Also be sure to study your photo as you finish each of the last three exercises of this book, and spend time praising God for making you the gifted, talented person you are.

Prayer: Jesus, even in the darkest of days, keep Your eternal springtime alive in my heart.

Exercise 3

....

THANKFUL THINGS

When the Lord saw her, his heart went out to her and he said, "Don't cry."
Luke 7:13, NIV

A book was loaned to me not too many months ago. The author, a Christian, had won national recognition. His book was absorbing, inspirational, personal, but the story it told was a sad one. Still such bright hope shone through the tragedy the book chronicled that it left my heart about to burst with the joy of it.

Impetuously, I wrote the author, not daring to hope that I'd hear from him in return, but, for some reason waiting and feeling that he might respond. He did. And the thoughts expressed in his correspondence carried all the magic and inspiration of his book. We eventually met for an afternoon conversation. Never again have I experienced moments that had the shape and effect of those spent with him. Afterward, I realized that the afternoon—and the book that inspired it—had been a very special gift to me from God.

In the bright sunshine of a newborn day, in the fresh gentle rain, or in the stark coldness of the earth swept clean with snow, there's evidence of His love. Into each evening, we bring from our day that for which we can be thankful: a warm fire, a new friend, a plot of earth, a good book, and time, for a while, to read.

Whatever your life circumstances are at this moment, God has you where He wants you to be. As a Christian now is your sowing time, and, if you sow to the spirit and not the flesh, you will reap plentiful blessings in God's time. To grow toward God's likeness and become more and more filled with His life—is to grow in joy. You can now put aside the discouragement, defeat, bitterness, insecurity, fears and self-doubts. God will, in His great compassion, bring roses out of the sadness of your life. In the radiant joy of His presence, you can be assured that no matter what happens, He will be with you and there would be fresh flowers and new sunrises for each day. Rejoice, Christian, life everlasting is a joyful harvest indeed!

Living Free

Write a detailed description of a time when God brought joy out of a sorrowful situation in your life. Describe the emotions you felt before and after joy:

Prayer: Father, help me to recognize the flowers and the bright new sunrises that You bring into my day. Lift my spirit in praise for the joy You place in my heart.

Exercise 4

....

A TRIBUTE

Be careful that you do not forget the LORD, who brought
you out of Egypt, out of the land of slavery.
Deuteronomy 6:12, NIV

Remind me of Your presence, Father, as I go on with my life. You're the source of all good things in it. Without You, there would be no purpose in ministry, no reason to offer hope to others. You have brought me out of the slavery of sin. You have salvaged my soul and grasped me by the hands to pull me from the quagmire of despair.

It was You who created the circumstances in which all that is good in me could reach for a breath of sunlight and win the struggle to survive and bear fruit. Life is good now, full of bright possibilities and exciting opportunities. Lord, let me not forget that it was You who brought me to this place. It was You who drew me closer to your breast and gently shaped my life so that it could bear flowers instead of thorns. Let these flowers now be a tribute to Your love and Your patience and Your prudent pruning of my life.

Experience has taught me only too keenly, Lord, that success, even in doing Your work, can tempt me to forget you. In moments when I'm most aware of the fruits of my labor, I take my eyes off of You and open my life to all sorts of unkind thoughts and jealous ambitions. Not so, at this moment, Lord. I long only to walk the path of life with You.

Take away from me any sinful thoughts and purify my soul. Free my heart from attachment to old ways and from guilt over past wrongs now forgiven. Set my mind on You and let all that I do spring from Your abiding love in my heart. Strengthen my faith until there's no longer room for doubt. Keep ever close to me, so that when I wake in the morning, I'm aware of Your presence; and when I retire at night, I do so knowing that we have walked this day together.

Spiritual Prep: *Deuteronomy 8:2; 1 Chronicles 16:12; Psalms 77:11–12; 103:1–5;*
Lamentations 3:21–23

Write your own tribute to God:

Prayer: My Lord and Father, I lift my tribute up to You.

Exercise 5

....

SONGS OF JOY

The LORD is my strength and my defense; he has become my salvation. He is my God,
and I will praise him, my father's God, and I will exalt him.
Exodus 15:2, NIV

Lord, let this be a song of praise
    for being a constant Friend,
        for cleansing me from all my sin,
            for patience with me through all my days,
                and healing me of errant ways,
for giving me a new life, touched by the Son;
for making my world, in all of its confusing reality, a joyful one.

You've blessed my life with purpose, filled it with love,
Guided me in peace—with the presence of Your Dove.

Father, let this be a song of praise
for all the times You've lifted me up to Your high place,
and rested me there in gentle and perfect grace.

Spiritual Prep: *Psalms 69:30; 95:1–3; 106:1–2; Revelation 7:12*

Living Free

Write out your own song of joy to the Lord for being His child, His beloved. Repeat or sing it as you study the adult photograph of yourself which you placed in this book.

Prayer: Regardless of what life brings, Lord Jesus, keep Your love and Your praise always in my heart.

Appendix: Leading an "All I'm Created to Be: Set Free" Small Group

Your role as small-group leader is to facilitate personal and spiritual growth in each member. It's not the intent of this book—or of your role as leader—to teach facts, theories, or ways of doing. What you are responsible for, as group leader, is to:

- Exercise patience, so that each session unfolds in a way that best helps group members.
- Trust in the Holy Spirit to guide the members to see and hear that which best meets their needs—and to accept that each member may encounter the Holy Spirit in different ways.
- Listen.
- Allow occasional silences. Give the rest of the group opportunities to process what they've heard.
- Affirm God's guidance and ways in which He speaks to each participant.
- In other words: No lecturing, controlling, or "fixing." Your "fix" or solution may not be God's solution for that person.

Group Leader Preparation

1. Spiritually: Always seek God's guidance as a group leader, and remain open to the Holy Spirit's guidance. Pray for each group member, and for your journey together.
2. Materially: You'll need . . .

- a confidential space in which to meet
- chairs
- desks or other writing surfaces
- group ground rules (see General Guidelines below), on flip chart or paper copies
- Bibles
- pens and/or pencils; All I'm Created to Be: Set Free books for each member
- a prayer-request notebook
- songs and musical accompaniment of some kind, if you wish to include singing

Ideally, you'll want to find a meeting area where confidentiality can be assured. Also, set up your chairs or desks in a circle or square, to encourage interaction between group members. At the same time, allow enough distance between individuals so that they have confidentiality while writing in their journals.

General Guidelines

1. Decide on a timeframe. You'll need one-and-a-half to two hours for each session. Less is not enough time to warm up, and more time than this creates stress and fatigue.

2. Confidentiality. What's said in the group stays in the group. Do not discuss what's shared with others outside the group.

3. Freedom of Participation. Opportunities for each member to verbally respond to Each question should be encouraged, but not demanded. Any individual has the freedom to "pass" on responding verbally to any of the questions in the workbook.

4. Form of Participation. Each member of the group needs to speak in first person ("I," "me," "my," "myself") only and not in second ("you") or third person ("they," "them").

5. Support—don't "fix." Discourage judging, "fixing," and dominating the group by Any participant. Do not allow interrupting, mocking, belittling, nor cross-talk (conversation between two people, excluding all others).

Again, these are basic rules and guidelines, but some form of these should be a part of your group's DNA. Adjust and adapt them as needed, to fit your group's needs.

Now you're ready to have your group time. With that, here's a general format for how to run your group, followed by some more specific recommendations for your opening and closing sessions. The below assumes that you're working within the hour-and-a-half to two-hour format. Again, adapt these to the needs of your group as needed:

Typical Meeting Agenda:

(Approximately one hour) Discuss one journaling question at a time, allowing participants to volunteer or "pass" on sharing their responses. Encourage feedback and sharing following each response.

(Approximately 15 minutes) Ask for prayer requests, and record them in your notebook. Allow volunteer prayer for these requests from group members.

Close, if you would like, with a song (group singing, CD, or instrumental)

EXAMPLE: WEEK ONE

Then you will know the truth, and the truth will set you free.
John 8:32, NIV

1. Write out and display the above verse (John 8:32) on a banner, poster, or flipchart.

2. Welcome each member as he or she arrives.

3. Open in prayer.

4. Begin by saying something like: "This meeting is preparation for a journey together in personal and spiritual growth. Tonight we'll spend time getting to know each other a little better and discussing the guidelines and expectations for the group."

5. Have each member introduce himself/herself by sharing:
   - his/her name
   - if they're in school, college, or where they work, and telling about their major or job
   - their favorite pastime
   - current family (including pets)

6. Restate that the purpose of the group is to work toward personal and spiritual growth as they share experiences, affirmations, and hope with each other. Encourage group members to claim John 8:23 as they work through the book and engage in the journaling. Also encourage them in the knowledge that God can free them from any hurts and hang-ups and give them a new freedom to experience His joy, His peace, and His love.

7. Hand out "All I'm Created to Be: Set Free" workbooks to everyone and go over the content with the group so that each member will understand the process of reading, "Spiritual prep," journaling, discussion, and prayer that will frame each session together. Emphasize that the journaling for each exercise is to be completed prior to coming to the group meeting.

8. Discuss materials needed. (See the "Group Leader Preparation" section above if needed.) Ask participants to bring Bibles, workbook, pencils, and open minds to each meeting.

9. Ask participants to complete the journaling parts, "All I'm Created to Be" and "Set Free" of Exercise 1 in Step 1 before your next meeting. Let your group member know that this will be the pattern going forward; each exercise will be completed at home prior to discussing that particular exercise in the group meeting.

10. Go over the group rules together. (Again, consult the General Guidelines section above as needed.) Make sure everyone understands and agrees with your group rules before moving on.

11. Brainstorm: Ask the following questions one at a time, and give time to record all responses on a flipchart or blackboard:
    a. What are your hopes and expectations for the time ahead of us in this group?
    b. What are your anxieties about this time together?

12. Focus: Read the author's introduction to the workbook.

13. Remind participants to complete the journaling portions of Step 1, Exercise 1 before the next meeting.

14. Start your "prayer-request" list. Say something like, "Prayer requests will be recorded by the leader. Each week we will spend some time as a group praying for the requests. Confidentiality applies here also. What is said in the group stays in the group, including the prayer requests."

15. Close your initial session in prayer, committing you hopes and fears from the brainstorming session to God. Also prayer for any requests mentioned.

EXAMPLE: WEEK TWO

Step 1
Exercise 1: Out from Behind the Mask

Note: Because each session will follow the same basic agenda—with any modifications that you, as leader, feel are needed—this agenda will be outlined only once.

1. Welcome group members, and open with prayer.
2. Leader reads aloud to the group the introductory story, in this case: Anna's story.
3. Read the opening Scripture verse: 1 Samuel 16:7
4. Spiritual Prep: Again, take one verse at a time. Let a group member read each verse, then take a little time as a group to react to it and how it pertains to this week's topic. For example:
   a. Psalm 51:6: God's desire for us involves what sort truth?
   b. John 7:24: This verse tells us not to judge by appearance, but according to "righteous judgment": What do you think the writer means by "righteous judgment?"
5. Ask if each person has completed the journaling section of Exercise One, "All I'm Created to Be" and "Set Free." If not, you may want to allow fifteen to twenty minutes for them to do so, but stress verbally that the journaling section should be completed before coming to the meeting.
6. Discuss each journal question one at a time. Go around the group, allowing each participant to either answer or "pass." Allow gentle questions and affirmative discussion as each participant shares his or her answer to each of the thought questions (not needed for the single-answer fact questions).
7. Once you're done with your journal discussion, allow a few more minutes afterward for general discussion of the topic.
8. Take prayer requests. As participants make requests, be sure to write them in your prayer notebook.
9. Close your group time in prayer and—and if you'd like, by singing and/or playing a worship song (on CD).

WEEKS 3–50

Continue to follow the above agenda, with modifications as you feel are needed or that you're led to make.

FINAL MEETING

Closure

1. Before your group time:
   - Prepare a double-spaced list of every participant in the group. Make enough copies of the list for each participant.
   - Also, bring several pairs of scissors to the meeting—enough for every two or three members to share a set. Set them up around your circle/square before your meeting time.
   - You'll also need one small bottle of glue.
   - Celebration Option: You may also wish to offer some sort of small certificate to each person who completes the program. This can be done in a very relaxed way, or in a more formal setting followed by a finger-food celebration.
2. Open with greeting and a prayer.
3. Do the following affirmation exercise together:
   a. Distribute a copy of the lists you prepared to each member of the group. Allow enough silent time for each member to write something they've come to like and/or admire about each person on the list.
   b. As people complete their lists of affirmations, have them cut the affirmations, each paired with the correct name, into strips—and have them hang onto their sets of strips afterward.
   c. Put one chair in the center of the circle—your "hot seat"—and put your bottle of glue next to it.
   d. Have one person at a time take the "hot seat." Give the person in the hot seat a bottle of glue, and have them open their workbooks to the last, blank page in the book.
   e. While the individual remains in the hot seat, each member of the group will read his/her affirmation of that person, and then give their strips of to the person in the hot seat. Give the person in the hot seat time to glue each strip of paper on to his/her blank workbook page.
   f. Go on to the next group member, and repeat the process until everyone's had a chance to sit in the hot seat and glue their strips of paper to their workbooks.
4. If you're doing the Celebration Option, present your certificates now, to further your celebration of each group member's accomplishment and contribution to the group. Allow time during or after your celebration for individual group members to share feedback on how helpful the program has been, how they feel about their own progress since beginning the program, and what improvements they'd like to see made to the program.
5. Close your time in prayer, thanking God for everything He's done through your group members, and for everything He has yet do in their lives.

Printed in the United States
By Bookmasters